THE PASTOR *and*

THE PATIENT

The PASTOR and the PATIENT

A Practical Guidebook for Hospital Visitation

KENT D. RICHMOND & DAVID L. MIDDLETON

ABINGDON PRESS
Nashville

THE PASTOR AND THE PATIENT:
A PRACTICAL GUIDEBOOK FOR HOSPITAL VISITATION

Copyright © 1992 by Abingdon Press

This book is printed on acid-free, recycled paper.

Library of Congress Cataloging-in-Publication Data
RICHMOND, KENT D., 1939–
    The pastor and the patient : a practical guidebook for hospital visitation / Kent D. Richmond, David L. Middleton.
    p.   cm.
    Includes bibliographical references.
    ISBN 0-687-30352-4 (alk. paper)
    1. Pastoral medicine. I. Middleton, David L., 1935– .
    II. Title.
    BV4335.R55   1992
    259'.4—dc20   92-5133
                                                                              CIP

MANUFACTURED IN THE UNITED STATES OF AMERICA

For
Dorothy Richmond and Vera Middleton
Partners in Ministry

"And now faith, hope, and love abide . . . and the greatest
of these is love."
—*I Corinthians 13:13*

CONTENTS

CONTENTS

PREFACE

THIS IS a volume about the pastor's hospital ministry. In the 25th chapter of the Gospel of Matthew, Jesus made it clear to his disciples that meaningful ministry in his name implied service to "the least of these who are members of [Jesus'] family" (25:40). He went on to identify such service with ministry to himself. Part of that ministry involves visiting the sick.

Little more than a generation ago, the sick could be found at home, either recuperating or passing the hours and days until death put an end to their suffering. Today, the sick and dying are found almost universally in an institutional setting. Whether it be nursing home, hospice, or hospital, it is incumbent on the pastor that she take seriously the call to bring comfort to those who are sick. There are many volumes that provide guidance to the pastor in carrying out this aspect of parish ministry. Some of those titles can be found in the bibliography appended to the end of this book.

This volume is different in several ways. First, it is written from the inside out. Both of its authors are hospital chaplains who have served as parish pastors. We have our feet in both camps. We are aware of the tasks of the parish pastor; we are also aware of the nature of the hospital setting in which the pastor must carry out ministry to the sick. Second, as hospital chaplains, we are engaged in the subject about which we write. The volume is illustrated by incidents that come directly from the hospital setting. Third, since both of us are involved in ministry in a large metropolitan acute-care institution, which is also a level-one trauma center, we feel that we are able to bring insights into hospital ministry not necessarily present in volumes written by those who stand outside the hospital setting. Finally, one of us is certified for the supervision and training of pastors by the Association for Clinical Pastoral Education (ACPE), and is director of CPE at our hospital. CPE has virtually become a prerequisite for conducting hospital ministry today. Many denominations require one or more quarters of such training before committing to ordination. It is our hope that this book benefits from that area of expertise as well.

A word about organization. Our mandate for caring comes from the ministry of Jesus and it is incumbent upon us to hold a sound theological understanding of that foundation. The first chapter attempts to prepare the ground. Chapter 2 invites us to understand the origin of the hospital and the significant changes that have virtually revolutionized health care and pastoral ministry in the health care institution. Chapters 3 and 4 examine the theological and ethical homework that must be done by the pastor as preparation for effectively carrying out hospital ministry. Chapter 5 attempts to offer advice to the pastor that can help him gain entry to the hospital and information about his patient. It is written out of a deep conviction that the pastor is an essential member of the team of caregivers who attempt to bring healing to a patient. The sixth chapter examines the hopes, fears, and needs that are presented by a number of different kinds of patients. It is offered in the hope that it will significantly help the visiting pastor better understand the dynamics of illness and ministry to patients who bring particularly tragic or complex circumstances to their illness. Chapter 7 looks in depth at the spiritual resources that the pastor can bring to such patients. Chapter 8 recognizes that, although patients leave the hospital, ministry does not necessarily cease upon discharge. A number of programs exist for helping the pastor assist her parishioners in continued healing. Finally, the last chapter attempts to hold up the dynamics entering into successful pastoral communication with patients who are sick. As such, it brings a number of helpful insights out of the field of clinical pastoral education. It is our hope that this chapter will assist the pastor to hear more effectively the patient's needs and speak to them.

Although this book is the joint effort of two authors, each of us is primarily responsible for individual chapters. Chapters 1, 2, 5, 8, and 9 are written by David Middleton. Kent Richmond is the writer of chapters 3, 4, 6, and 7.

There are a number of persons whose influence has touched our lives, and, though responsibility for the content of this volume lies with its authors, we would be remiss if we did not express a word of thanks to those whose thought has helped us.

We are grateful to the parishioners, patients, and students who have enriched our understanding of pastoral care through shared experiences. We particularly remember our teachers Carrol Wise and Wayne Oates, pioneers in the field of pastoral care.

To Thelma Rudy, who helped to type part of the manuscript, must go a word of appreciation. Thelma is more than secretary for the CPE department at Lutheran General. She is a friend to staff and students.

Our colleagues on the staff of the pastoral care department at Lutheran General Hospital are a constant source of challenge and learning. Behind the banter we share, there is a faithful commitment to incarnating the love of God, not only for the patients whom we serve but also for one another.

A word of thanks must go to the editorial staff at Abingdon Press: to Professional Books Editor, Paul Franklyn, who conceived of this book and shepherded it along, and to Steve Cox, whose copyediting skill helped to make the book readable.

Finally, David would like to thank his father, Carl Middleton, a retired General Baptist pastor, at whose side David first became aware of how deeply and compassionately persons can be loved through hospital ministry.

THE PASTOR *and* THE PATIENT

CHAPTER ONE

A PASTORAL THEOLOGY

Biblical and Theological Foundations for Visiting the Hospitalized Parishioner

I was sick and you took care of me,
I was in prison and you visited me.
—Matthew 25:36 NRSV

THE VISITATION of the sick is a well-established practice of pastoral ministry. It is commonly expected that pastors will visit parishioners who are hospitalized. Unfortunately, such common expectations may lead to unexamined work that is done out of a sense of duty. Obligatory pastoral visitation may become routine.

Most of us resist routine, obligatory tasks. We struggle with ourselves, procrastinate, and push ourselves to do what has to be done. Then our visits may lack a sense of purpose and seem pointless. We visit our parishioners but are not sure why. We feel out of place in the hospital and are not sure what we are doing there.

Pastoral visitation of the sick is but one part of pastoral care. So we begin with a review of images that give direction to pastoral ministry, by examining those images and theological concepts as they lend meaning or motivation to visitation of sick parishioners in the hospital.

THE SHEPHERD

The word *pastor* is derived from the image of the shepherd. This image is abundant in the scriptures of the Old and New Testaments. No other metaphor has so influenced our understanding of pastoral ministry.

THE PASTOR AND THE PATIENT

When I think of the shepherd image, I recall from my childhood days in Sunday school the picture of a young shepherd on a steep and rugged slope. He was shown fully extended, reaching for a sheep that was isolated on a ledge. It was a dramatic visual portrayal of the parable of the lost sheep.

The parable of the lost sheep is a fitting image for the pastoral visitation of hospitalized parishioners. Many patients in the hospital are cut off from the security of their normal environment and find themselves in a potentially dangerous and often lonely situation. The pastor (shepherd) leaves the ninety-nine secure parishioners to reach out to the one who is endangered.

THE INCARNATION

Our pastoral visitation has a representative function. In visiting the sick person the pastor re-presents the presence and the loving care of God in the person of Christ the Good Shepherd. The guiding theological perspective is that of incarnation. As pastors we "enflesh" the body of Christ. According to Henri Nouwen, we serve as living reminders of Jesus Christ.[1]

This incarnational perspective informs our pastoral identity. According to Herbert Anderson, the pastor "gains internal legitimation through identification with Jesus. If indeed my body is Christ's body, then my being . . . in the hospital room is authenticated through identification with Christ. Embodying Christ means literally that I understand my body to be a means of grace. The transforming love of God is made known by my presence."[2]

This incarnational identification with Jesus Christ has some pitfalls, which Anderson is careful to point out. It can lead to exaggerating the authority or power of the pastor over that of the sick parishioner. A faulty understanding of incarnational theology can tempt both pastor and parishioner toward a denial of human finitude and limits. Jesus was tempted to prove his "Godlikeness" by turning stones into bread and demonstrate his power by defying his mortality (Matthew 4:1-11). Just as Jesus refused to conform with the heroic messianic expectations of his people, so pastors have to struggle with messianic expectations of themselves and their people.

If we cater to the exaggerated expectations of others, we will promise more than we can deliver and encourage expectations that may not be met. We are in danger of idolatry and should remember that idols fall when they fail to meet the unrealistic expectations of their worshipers. It is understandable that persons

in distress, overwhelmed by their powerlessness or terrified of death, want us to have more answers than we know. They want our presence to be able to take away the terror of being small. They want to be assured that our prayers have more influence than theirs. . . . This is a perennial trap for pastoral care. There is something beguiling about being a buffer. And if we have already identified our body with Christ's body, we are in double jeopardy.[3]

Another drawback of overidentifying the pastor's presence with the incarnation of Christ is that of focusing too narrowly on the individual at the expense of ignoring the corporate nature of the body of Christ. The body of Christ is continued through the church, and we are individually only members of the whole body of Christ. There are two implications of this corporate understanding of incarnational theology for the practice of pastoral care.

First, as pastors we not only individually represent Christ but we also represent the church as the body of Christ, the community of faith. By our presence in the hospital room, we remind people not only of the caring presence of God. We also remind them that they are part of a community of faith that cares for them and embodies the loving care of God. A pastor represents the whole church of God. Each pastor also represents a particular congregation and extends the congregation's support to the isolated parishioner who may experience separation from both God and the community of faith. The pastor becomes the living reminder that God and church are present.

Second, to claim incarnational identity as the exclusive possession of the caregiver is to deny the incarnation of Christ in the patient. It magnifies the power of the pastor as it diminishes the importance of the parishioner. Paul Tillich perceived this as a fundamental problem and wrote that, when he imagined himself to be the recipient of pastoral care, he somehow felt humiliated. "Someone else makes me an object of his care, but no one wants to become an object and, therefore, . . . resists such situations like pastoral care."

Being hospitalized for illness is a reductive experience. Persons are made the objects of other persons' care and thereby feel diminished. Tillich advocated that "the basic principle for the attitude of pastoral [care] is mutuality."[4]

A theological basis for mutuality can be found in perceiving Christ in the person of the suffering patient. This very incarnational perspective is suggested in Jesus' story of the judgment of the nations in Matthew 25:31-46.

The Son of Man . . . will separate people one from another as a shepherd separates the sheep from the goats. . . . Then the king will say to those at his right hand, "Come . . . inherit the kingdom . . . for I was hungry and you gave me food, I was thirsty and you gave me something to drink, I was a stranger and you welcomed me, I was naked and you gave me clothing, I was sick and you took care of me, I was in prison and you visited me."

The reply to the question of the righteous, "Lord, when was it" that we saw you in these conditions and did these things for you, was, "Truly I tell you, just as you did it to one of the least of these who are members of my family, you did it to me."

This passage suggests that the one to whom we minister truly embodies the suffering Christ, and in our pastoral care of the "least of these" we are indeed ministering to Christ and serving the needs of Christ himself. This is the incarnational viewpoint expressed in the following letter addressed to Elector Frederick of Saxony by Martin Luther.

When, therefore, I learned, most illustrious prince, that Your Lordship has been afflicted with a grave illness and that Christ has at the same time become ill in you, I counted it my duty to visit Your Lordship with a little writing of mine. I cannot pretend that I do not hear the voice of Christ crying out to me from Your Lordship's body and flesh and saying, "Behold, I am sick." This is so because such evils as illness and the like are not borne by us who are Christians but by Christ himself, our Lord and Saviour, in whom we live.[5]

The perception of the patient as the locus of the incarnation and that as fellow members of the body of Christ we all share in the incarnation serves as a corrective to appropriating the concept of the incarnation as the exclusive prerogative of pastors. It suggests a mutuality of relationships that recognizes our common humanity and finitude. It prevents the distancing that places the pastor in the superior position of one who "lords it over" the parishioner as if beyond the limitations and failings common to all humanity.

The base from which we offer pastoral care is one that shares in the incarnation. We minister as fellow pilgrims who share the finitude, the limitations, the mortality, the failings, the struggles, and the sinfulness of all humanity. We serve in the name of the One who took our humanity upon himself and has become acquainted with our sorrows and our griefs. He has experienced and continues to experience our powerlessness with us.

We re-present the one who leads us beside still waters and restores our souls, the great shepherd who walks with us through life's darkest valley, that of the shadow of death.

THE NATURE OF THE PASTORAL RELATIONSHIP

The first, and most important, implication of the shepherd image for the pastoral visitation of the hospitalized parishioner is relational. The nature of that relationship is one that involves familiarity, caring, and initiative.

Familiarity

The shepherd knows the sheep and the sheep recognize the shepherd's voice (John 10:4). Jesus said, "I am the good shepherd. I know my own and my own know me" (John 10:14).

THE PASTOR AND THE PATIENT

The pastor's relationship with the parishioner extends beyond the perimeters of hospitalization. A pastor knows the patient in other circumstances and in a variety of situations. The pastor, better than the hospital personnel, knows what patients are like under more normal, less threatening circumstances.

A hospitalized parishioner is lost or caught in a strange and threatening place. While medical personnel may be caring people, they tend to relate to patients as the *objects* of care and focus specifically on their diseases, treatments, and vital signs. To them a parishioner may have become the "M.I. [heart patient] in room 10," or the "CVA [stroke patient] in bed 3." While it is hoped that medical personnel relate to patients as persons, it is essential that they relate to them as objects of care. That is what Martin Buber referred to as an "I-it" quality of these relationships. Such a style of relating can be so disorienting that patients feel lost, diminished, and out of touch. It is depersonalizing.

The pastor's visit can serve as a powerful corrective to this tendency. A pastor comes as one who knows the patient as a whole person, not only as a sick person, and certainly not as a disease. It is a powerful reminder to patients that they are persons of worth. The pastor is the one person who enters their room and does not have to *do* something to them. They are not the objects of our treatment. We offer them a relationship that has an "I-thou" quality to it. It is a powerful reminder of Whose they are and therefore who they are. They are fully human beings, children of God, created in the image of God.

Pastors must be reminded of the importance of this relational quality—throughout their ministry. Pastors and students in clinical pastoral education often envy physicians and nurses because medical personnel have specific, clearly structured tasks. They seem to have a clearer understanding of what they are *doing* and can often see the measurable results of their efforts. But the personhood of the patient may be lost on the precipitous slopes of health care, and an effective pastoral visit can help the lost parishioner to find her place again. Because we have been present with parishioners and will continue to be with them in other, more secure places, our physical presence with them in this time and place gives them more security and helps lessen the panic and anxiety. Someone they know is with them and is a powerful, living reminder of the One who has promised never to leave them or forsake them (Hebrews 13:5)—the Lord who is our shepherd and is with us "even though [we] walk through the darkest valley (Psalm 23)."

A pastoral visit helps people to stay in touch with that which is familiar, with their place in relationship to God and the community of faith. It helps to keep them in touch with that which "restores their souls" and strengthens them in their faith.

Caring

The pastoral relationship that emerges from the image of the good shepherd is described in terms of caring. In Ezekiel 34, God is described as the true Shepherd of Israel who *cares* for the sheep. "I myself will be the shepherd of my sheep, and I will make them lie down, says the Lord God. I will seek the lost, and I will bring back the strayed, and I will bind up the injured, and I will strengthen the weak" (Ezekiel 34.15-16).

Again it is the primacy of *caring* that distinguishes the pastoral visit from those of medical personnel of the hospital community. Though they also may be caring people, their efforts are focused primarily on curing. As medicine has become more effective, the shift from caring to curing has intensified in hospitals. When it is determined that a cure is no longer possible for a given patient, a crisis point is reached. The doctor may conclude, "There is nothing else we can do." That simply means there is nothing else that can be done to bring about a cure. Of course there is still palliative treatment. The patient can be made more comfortable. Care can still be provided. The patient is no longer an object to be repaired or a problem to be solved. There is still a person in need of supportive relationships—a ministry of presence.

Increasingly in a cost-conscious world, a discharge will be considered at the point when the shift is made from curing to caring. Patients may be discharged to a hospice, a nursing home, or referred to a home care program. It is at this point that some patients and their families feel abandoned and that no one *really* cares for them.

The caring of the good shepherd, the pastor, goes beyond the perimeters of healing and curing. It conveys a faithful relationship that reaches beyond the failure of efforts to cure. It embodies the love of Christ from which "neither death, nor life, nor angels, nor rulers, nor things present, nor things to come, nor powers, nor height, nor depth, nor anything else in all creation" can separate us (Romans 8:38-39). Our pastoral caring serves as a living reminder of the everlasting care of the Good Shepherd.

Pastoral Initiative

In a shepherding relationship the pastor seeks after the lost. The Good Shepherd searches out the strayed, the lost, and the fallen. The pastoral act of visiting a parishioner in the hospital communicates that seeking quality of God.

This seeking characteristic provides the imaginative basis for the practice of pastoral initiative. The right of initiative is unique to the pastoral role. Other professions do not claim it as a right. In fact, in the practice of other professions, it might well be considered unethical.

Initiative is a mixed blessing for pastors. Pastors may feel that their uninvited visits are intrusive. There is certainly an ambiguous quality and perhaps a presumptuous quality to initiating a visit not explicitly requested. As pastors we can only anticipate what some of the reactions might be. It is no wonder that clinical pastoral education students and many pastors are reluctant to initiate such visits.

Pastoral initiative suggests the covenant nature of the relationship between pastor and parishioner. As a member of the church, the body of Christ, the parishioner has entered into a relationship with a community of faith and care. That care is personified in the person of the pastor. Implicit in this covenant is the parishioner's willingness to receive the care of a seeking God through the care of others.

Seward Hiltner addressed this covenant perspective for pastoral initiative.

A PASTORAL THEOLOGY

Central to the content of shepherding is the shepherd's solicitous concern for the welfare of the sheep. The most basic attitude of the pastor does not vary from one situation to another, although it assumes different forms from the point of view of others in the situation. To the notion of shepherding as solicitude in the pastor, therefore, *we must add the necessary presence of some degree of recognition of need to the parishioner and some degree of receptivity to help.* The need . . . is always specific, although the recognition of its nature need not be clear and distinct.[6] (emphasis added)

The crisis of the parishioner may have immobilized the quest for help. Some may assume that the pastor will take initiative in crisis situations and that their own call for help is not necessary. When the pastor takes the initiative, the visibility so provided may encourage the parishioner to make use of the care that is offered.

PASTORAL FUNCTIONS

In addition to the nature of the relationship between pastor and parishioner, the shepherd motif suggests three pastoral operations that are relevant to pastoral visitation in the hospital setting. The shepherd's job description can be divided into three functions. The shepherd guided the flock beside still waters and into green pastures, gave them sustenance, and bound up their wounds.

These three aspects of shepherding have been categorized as *healing, sustaining,* and *guiding.* Although there is some overlapping in these three pastoral operations, there are characteristics that distinguish them and make each necessary. "If we had only healing, it might wrongly be assumed that all wounds could be bound up, would heal, and that the focal infection in any situation could always be cured or changed in essence, which plainly is not true."[7]

Healing

Healing is defined as the restoration of a functional wholeness that has been lost or delayed. In biblical imagery the shepherd bound up the wounds and supported the processes of healing.

From a Christian point of view, all healing is of God. God works in various ways and through the gifts and skills of different people. God's efforts are not excluded from so-called "secular" forms of healing. Nor is God confined to those specific ways of healing that are identified as religious or Christian. The work of healing is a joint effort and not an arena for competing claims. The Christian pastor has an appropriate place on the healing team.

Henri Nouwen suggests that the healing work of pastors as living reminders is in helping people to tell, accept, and understand their own stories as they fit into God's story of salvation.

The challenge of ministry is to help people in very concrete situations—people with illnesses or in grief, people with physical or mental handicaps, people suffering from poverty and oppression, people caught in the complex networks of secular or religious institutions—to see and experience their story as part of God's ongoing redemptive work in the world. These insights and experiences heal precisely because they restore the broken connection between the world and God and create a new unity in which memories that formerly seemed only destructive are now reclaimed as part of a redemptive event.[8]

As people experience God's grace through their pastor, they experience healing as well.

It is helpful to remember that healing is only one of the pastoral functions, and it is not always the appropriate one. Many come to pastoral ministry with the illusion that all persons can be healed, restored to wholeness. This may lead to a narrow focus in ministry in which it is assumed that all human problems have a solution and the pastor is the "repairman" who can fix anything. A preoccupation with "people fixing" or curing deprives people of the full range of pastoral care, and the pastor may become frustrated and feel ineffective.

There is another fairly common error in the practice of pastoral healing. Even when the healing function is appropriate, the pastor's need to help may be excessive. We may assume too much responsibility for the care of another and deny their responsible participation in their own recovery. Such an approach encourages unnecessary dependency, which can be destructive.

In our zeal to do good we may not act wisely. Jesus demonstrated wisdom in his healing of the lame man near the pool of Bethzatha. He began by inviting the man's participation with the question, "Do you want to be made well?" (John 5:6). Jesus clearly exercised pastoral initiative, but he transferred the initiative by inviting the man's response. Perhaps Jesus knew that disease can have its secondary benefits. He did not impose his healing ministry upon another without that person's permission.

Later in the story Jesus again encouraged the man to take responsibility and participate in his own recovery when he said to him, "Stand up, take your mat and walk" (John 5:8). The man had been ill for thirty-eight years. He had well-established patterns of dependency that needed to be addressed seriously.

Sustaining

The second shepherding function is sustaining. According to Hiltner, sustaining "is that aspect of the shepherding perspective that emphasizes 'standing by.' "[9] This is the supportive, comforting (encouraging) function of pastoral ministry. To reverse an old adage, it is the time when the pastor must say, "Don't just do something, stand there!" It is the time when the shepherd walks with the frightened and lonely through the dark and frightening places. It is the ministry of "being with" the afflicted in their helplessness, powerlessness, when they are hurting and frightened, helping them to find strength in knowing they are not alone. This is the pastoral function that is called for in bereavement. It is the ministry provided in the face of immediate trauma or in the midst of a crisis.

It takes the courage of faith to be with people in the midst of their pain, their fear, and their helplessness. The temptation is always present to avoid these situations. One way we avoid the sense of helplessness is to escape the feelings of the present by refocusing on the future. We give untimely assurances that everything will be fine, that the situation will improve in time. We may make trivial the harshness of reality and the intensity of people's feelings by assuring them that the situation is not as bad as it appears, or observing that it could be worse. We may cite scriptures in support of all of this hollow reassurance.

The common pattern in all false reassurance is that it skips over, or attempts to evade, present reality. Dietrich Bonhoeffer once said that genuine reassurance is a matter of timing. He said there is a time to speak the ultimate word of hope. We can speak it with real faith and conviction only when we have been with people in and through the penultimate of their experience. We cannot speak the ultimate word of hope with authenticity in a penultimate time.

Once I entered a patient's room, noticed that she had been crying, and introduced myself as the chaplain. She responded by saying, "I really need a chaplain right now. Please don't leave me. Less than an hour ago the doctor came in and told me I had cancer and it is terminal. I was crying when my pastor walked in. He said, 'Hi, I see you are upset. I'll come back and visit with you when you are feeling better.' " What she needed was to be sustained in her crisis. Instead she felt that her pastor had abandoned her in a moment of extreme vulnerability. At that moment he failed theologically in re-presenting the faithful presence of a God who has promised not to abandon us in our time of need.

Guiding

The third shepherding function is *guiding*. As a shepherd leads the sheep through the wilderness, so the pastor leads parishioners through the desert places in their spiritual journeys. Hospitalization can be understood as a wilderness experience in the life of a person.

Moses served as a shepherd to the Israelites as he led them through their sojourn in the wilderness. The exodus was a crisis that shaped and changed the people of Israel. Hospitalization may be such a life changing and shaping event in the experience of our parishioner. The pastor's task is to guide patients through their wilderness.

We give guidance when people lose their sense of direction or purpose and find their way difficult. Hospitalization is a disorienting experience. In illness people raise questions about the meaning of their experience, the purpose of their suffering. Where does God fit into it? Hospitalized persons often become reflective and engage in self-examination and reassessment. Illness can be a time of changing values. Patients do not need authoritarian and specific answers from the pastor, nor do they need advice. They need a person who knows the terrain, who can provide guidance for their search.

Seward Hiltner considered the guiding function potentially the most abusive one. Under the facade of guidance, the pastor may impose individual views on the parishioner. Guidance can degenerate into coercion.

There are two primary ways in which the pastor serves as a guide to the hospitalized patient. First, the pastor helps the parishioner function as a theologian. The pastor may assist the parishioner who searches for meaning to understand the experience of suffering from a theological perspective. Second, the pastor's guidance may be appreciated while making moral choices about treatment. Decisions about advance directives, orders not to resuscitate, cessation of treatment, termination of pregnancy require a review of values. Often these values have not been clearly articulated. The pastor can provide valuable assistance in the search for the source of one's values through the implications of one's religious teachings. This may involve the sharing of information as well as guidance through the processes of decision making. The guidance the pastor can offer regarding moral issues in medicine will be covered in some detail in chapter 4.

All three aspects of the shepherding perspective meet the general requirements of pastoral care. Hiltner defined these requirements as having the following characteristics: "The situation is such that the shepherd's solicitous concern for the welfare of the persons is dominant, there is some degree of recognition of need within the persons, and there is some degree of receptivity to help."[10]

We have established the theological foundation for hospital ministry. We must now look more specifically at the modern hospital, in order to understand its origins and the changes that have shaken its very foundations.

CHAPTER TWO

THE HOSPITAL COMMUNITY

THE MODERN hospital is a living organism. The hospital is more than the place to which people go to earn their living. Because hospital personnel are in the business of caring for the sick and the dying, they may as a group be more in touch with human emotion. When a patient dies, nurses may weep along with family members. When a patient refuses to cooperate in his treatment, physicians become frustrated at their inability to help a patient see what is best for him. When a terminally ill patient expresses a desire to die, pastors and chaplains are moved and humbled as they accompany such a patient through that time. The hospital is a place of feeling, of movement, and as is always the case when people are involved, the hospital community is a place of change.

We live not only in changing times but in a time when change is accelerating. This is certainly true in the field of health care. Much of the change can be seen as drastic measures for containing the rapidly increasing costs of health care generally and hospitalization in particular. Efforts to control costs are changing the way people are admitted, treated, and discharged by hospitals.

The dramatic changes in health care practice require adjustments in the way we carry out pastoral care in the setting of the hospital. Some of the influences are obvious and others are more subtle. Although the setting of the hospital and cultural attitudes do not determine the purpose of pastoral care, they do influence the approach to pastoral care and require adaptive measures by the pastor.

ORIGIN OF THE HOSPITAL: FROM CARING TO CURING

The recent changes in health care can be seen in relation to a long historical shift from caring to curing. Christians established the first hospitals primarily to *care* for the *incurably* diseased. Today, a hospital without a mission to cure is all but inconceivable. In the early days of the Christian movement, however, lepers were seen as incurable and contagious and were treated as social outcasts. The church countered that social reality of the day not by offering a cure but by providing for care through hospitality. Historian Will Durant wrote, "The outstanding moral distinction of the Church was her extensive provision of charity."[1]

The Christian belief that human beings were created in God's image, particularly viewed in the light of the Incarnation, had two important consequences. . . . The first was the impetus it gave to Christian benevolence. . . . It was Christian concern for all persons, who bore God's image, particularly for those who were in need, that led to the establishment of the first hospitals in the fourth century.[2]

In fact, as Will Durant said, "The Church or her rich laymen founded public hospitals on a scale never known before."[3] One of those early hospitals was the first created for leprosy. It was established at Caesaria in Cappadocia about 372 c.e. by Basil the Great, who was the bishop of the area. It became a model for other hospitals. Gregory of Nazianzus left a description of this original hospital:

Go forth from the city, and behold a new city, the treasure house of godliness . . . in which disease is investigated and sympathy provided. . . . We have no longer to look on the tearful and pitiable sight of men like corpses before death, with limbs dead (from leprosy), driven

from cities, from dwellings, from public places, from water courses. . . .
Basil it was more than anyone who persuaded those who are men not to
scorn men, nor to dishonor Christ the head of all by their inhumanity
towards human beings.[4]

Early hospitals began with a perspective of caring rather than of
curing. A significant change in attitude gradually took place as
church and society began to accommodate a scientific approach to
health and medicine.

As scientific medicine, symbolized by the germ theory of disease,
gathered momentum in the nineteenth century, supernatural explanations
of disease increasingly gave way to naturalistic ones, and the commonly
shared values of medicine rather than distinctive religious beliefs more
and more determined attitudes toward sickness and health.[5]

As medicine's effectiveness in conquering disease improved,
"The Church and its hospitals began to identify with this curing
model, and persons in both medicine and ministry took on
therapeutic self-images."[6]

The church may have accommodated this model without
sufficient critical examination. While there were considerable
gains in the alliance between church and science, and the cause of
health and healing was immeasurably advanced, the concept of
caring was narrowed. As medicine shifted from art to science, the
role of the physician became more that of applied scientist. The
arts and humanities of medicine diminished. The patient became
more objectified and the relationship between patient and
caregiver became more impersonal. Then specialization began,
which further separated the physician from a holistic view of the
patient. Ironically, as medicine increased in its ability to cure, it
became less personal, less human, and less caring.

One of the ironic reversals in the history of health care is seen in
the hospice movement. With the intense emphasis on cure, it
became increasingly difficult to treat compassionately the
incurable, dying patient. Therefore separate institutions and
programs were established so that dying patients could be given

compassionate care without the intense efforts to cure them. The hospices are in principle very much like the original hospital for lepers.

Against this backdrop of a changing approach to medicine, with its shift from caring to curing, have come more recent and familiar changes, the impact of which is being felt in the hospital setting and is requiring changes in how pastors conduct hospital ministry. Changes include expansion of health care facilities, development of technology, and attempts to curtail the costs of health care.

The modern hospital has become intensely focused on treating the acutely ill; it is highly specialized and is technologically oriented. The loss of the personal element in medicine has been recognized as a problem, and attempts have been made to recover the art and humanness of medicine. In the 1970s, several medical schools began placing greater emphasis on the place of the humanities in medicine. Emphasis was made on working with dying patients, human sexuality, ethical issues, and communication.

In 1872 there were only 178 hospitals in the United States. By 1910 there were more than four thousand! Further expansion was initiated by the Hospital Survey and Construction Act (the Hill-Burton Bill) of 1946. Following World War II, Congress directed the surplus funds of a post-war economy to the building of hospitals. Hospitals were made available to smaller communities. Most of the hospital construction in the fifties and sixties was subsidized by Hill-Burton funds, either through grants or low-interest loans. From the passage of the Hill-Burton Bill in 1946 to 1973, 12 billion dollars were spent on hospital construction, and 403,000 beds were added, doubling the nation's hospital bed capacity.

THE HOSPITAL AS A BUSINESS: RISING HEALTH CARE COSTS

This tremendous expansion in hospital construction contributed to the increasing costs of health care. Further adding to the cost were two other changes. One was a ruling that hospital employees were entitled to a minimum wage. Prior to 1970 hospital workers were exempted from the minimum wage law and were underpaid. For a service industry deep in personnel, the change resulted in a drastic increase in costs.

A similar cost increase came as the result of rising insurance premiums during the seventies and into the eighties. Dissatisfied patients increasingly resorted to malpractice suits resulting in massive judgments. Premiums for insurance escalated with costs being passed on to consumers through rising room rates. Multiple increases of $25 to $40 in daily room rates were not untypical.

Doctors, fearing malpractice suits, began practicing "defensive medicine." They ordered more tests and required more documentation in order to protect themselves in the event of litigation. One good result of this increased concern has been the establishment of standards of practice for medical care.

Medicare for the elderly and Medicaid for the poor were incorporated into the Social Security Act of 1965. In 1967, the cost of these government-supported expenditures for health care approached $5 billion. By the mid 1980s they had grown to $57.3 billion. These changes have continued to escalate the costs of health care, resulting in reactive attempts by government and third-party payors to control the costs.

By the mid 1970s, a demand had grown to curtail the costs of health care services, which had risen to $322 billion. From 1950 to 1970, medical expenditures increased by 400 percent. The Secretary of Health, Education, and Welfare found that there was an excess of 200,000 hospital beds and noted that costs were escalating at an annual rate of 14 percent. It was also discovered that there were many patients whose treatment did not require hospitalization.

An important change was made in the delivery of health care services. Prior to the mid 1980s Medicare paid for treatment retrospectively. That is, payment was made in response to the hospital billing. During the 1980s Medicare shifted to a prospective plan of reimbursement. Accordingly, all medicare patients were assigned to one of 467 diagnostic related groups (DRG), based on the nature of the illness for which they were admitted to the hospital. Medicare established a fixed rate of reimbursement for the treatment of each illness. Every hospital now knows "up front" what it will receive from Medicare. If it can treat the patient for less than that, it makes money. If it cannot, the hospital loses money. Commercial insurors have followed suit. Health Management Organizations (HMO) set limits, negotiate with hospitals for the lowest rates, and follow similar plans of prospective payment.

Hospitals responded to this change in reimbursement by eliminating services considered nonessential or cost-ineffective. One result was the rapid expansion of highly advertised programs for the chemically dependent in the mid 1980s. By the end of the decade, however, the same regulations began to apply to these centers, and cutbacks and closings have begun in that sector as well.

The trend, then as now, was cost containment. Slogans of "do more with less" soon gave way to reductions in staff and services. A business mentality took over, with an eye on the "bottom line" and marketability. Hospitals became competitive, and the language of marketing became dominant.

One primary result of this effort to reduce the cost of health care has been to shorten the length of stay. Hospitals now have some program of "utilization review," which monitors length of stay and encourages physicians to consider early discharge.

Other practices that have contributed to cost effectiveness are "same day admissions" for surgery, effecting more treatment on an outpatient or ambulatory basis, eliminating expensive or questionable diagnostic testing, and early discharge to other treatment facilities such as a convalescence center or home care.

At the beginning of the 1990s, there is also a shortage of nurses. It is not that there are fewer nurses than during the 1980s when nursing schools and programs were being reduced. In fact there are more nurses and fewer patients in the hospital. But the patients are more seriously ill and require more nursing care and more outpatient and home care services. Advancing technology also requires more nurses.

Hospital staffs are caring for patients who are more acutely ill and require more intense treatment. Patient care has become more intensively task-oriented and less casual and personal. The president of one hospital expressed his concern that hospitals would become "body shops," indistinguishable from one another. Another hospital president observed that hospitals have become essentially enlarged intensive care units.

The work of medical social workers is increasingly restricted to that of discharge planning. Because of the shortened stay, discharge planning begins with admission. Because of early discharges, many patients are transferred to other institutions such as a hospice, rehabilitation, or convalescence center. Others are provided with some kind of home care arrangement. This allows the social worker less time to function as a personal or family counselor. There is also less time during which patients are available for conversation; because of shorter stays their time is more heavily taken by tests and treatment. Doctors, nurses, and therapists may be constantly checking vital signs, performing treatments, and taking the patient out for diagnostic tests and treatments, or patients may be medicated or in a stage of recovery that renders them unavailable. Finding the optimum time for visiting patients will be more difficult, and it may require more communication with the hospital staff.

Another trend in our society that is significant to the pastoral visitation of parishioners in the hospital is the growing concern for privacy. This concern has both attitudinal and legal dimensions. Laws in the past twenty years have restricted the personal information that can be made available without a person's written release. Current mental health code prohibits the hospital from notifying churches of the admission of patients for psychiatric or chemical dependency treatment.

Recent surveys of patients in several hospitals disclose a growing number of parishioners who do not want their pastors or congregations to be informed that they have been admitted to the hospital. Some patients reason that their illness is not that serious, that the pastor is too busy, or that the diagnosis is such that they do not want it to be made known. Of primary concern is that the information will be made public through the worship bulletin, church newsletter, or pulpit announcement.

Length of stay is another factor in notification. By the time the hospital notice reaches the pastor, the patient may very well have already been discharged. Increasingly pastors can rely less on hospital notification and will have to devise other systems to identify their hospitalized parishioners. Pastor and church must assume greater responsibility for obtaining this information.

IMPACT ON PASTORAL CARE

The overall result of these changes on the pastoral care of hospitalized patients is mixed. On the one hand the personal touch of a pastoral visit becomes even more important. On the other hand, as parishioners become less accessible, the opportunities for visitation in the hospital become more limited.

Pastoral care becomes more important because it offers an "I-thou" relationship in the midst of an increasingly depersonalized hospital experience. With the shortened length of stay, reduced personnel, and the more task-oriented approach of a high-tech hospital, patients are apt to feel even more objectified and lost. Pastoral visits and expressions of care help parishioners remain connected and more in touch with their own identity.

Practical suggestions for more effective pastoral care can be categorized in terms of admission, hospital stay, discharge, and post-discharge convalescence. These are the critical points for a parishioner who is hospitalized.

Admission-Preadmission

Parish notification of a parishioner's admission to the hospital is becoming increasingly less dependable. Attitudes about privacy, legal restraints, timing, and hospital costs all combine to make notification less reliable. Parishioners can be educated to take responsibility to inform their pastor of their hospitalization if they want a pastoral visit.

When the parishioner assumes more responsibility for communicating with the pastor, it gives the pastor a better opportunity to do some initial contracting for the nature of the pastoral care that is needed. Fortunately most hospital stays are scheduled in advance and allow for this kind of dialogue. A parishioner can inform the pastor of a pending admission, the reason for treatment, and some of the anticipatory concerns.

If a parishioner is being admitted for surgery, she can tell the pastor what it is for, if it is to be scheduled on the day of admission, or if it is to be performed on an outpatient basis. If outpatient or same-day surgery is planned, the pastor will have limited opportunity to visit the patient, and it will become increasingly advisable to consider a presurgical visit prior to admission. Pre-hospitalization visits may very well become a new standard of practice for pastors. Such a preadmission visit would allow the parishioner to divulge anxiety and anticipated concerns and allow the pastor to structure an unhurried, uninterrupted, pastoral visit with prayer and dialogue.

People who are scheduled to enter the hospital may frequently have anxiety and anticipatory concerns that are expressed either directly or indirectly. Often these concerns or anxieties are related to their mortality and feelings of vulnerability. These concerns call for a theological response.

Primary among such concerns is, What is going to happen to me? Will the diagnostic tests or the surgery uncover something very serious? A large number of people who enter the hospital have underlying fears of cancer or dying. There are secondary fears about separation, loneliness, loss of control, indignity, embarrassment, dependence, pain, loss of health, and a variety of other concerns that are common to us all. Increasingly people are anxious about the financial impact of hospitalization. An unrushed pastoral visit prior to admission may invite a parishioner to express and explore these fears and anxieties within a faithful pastoral relationship that can set those fears into a realistic framework.

Hospital Stay

Pastoral visits can often be timed around critical points. Some of these can be anticipated in advance and can be addressed in the preadmission visit. Following diagnostic tests, when a patient is likely to receive either encouraging or discouraging news and must make decisions about treatment, a visit from the pastor would be welcomed. For similar reasons a visit following surgery is in order. An early discharge with the possibility of being transferred to a nursing care facility or home care often arouses considerable anxiety for patient and family.

It is often helpful to be with a family and provide emotional and spiritual support during an operation. That need may be determined and contracted during a visit with the parishioner and family prior to the hospitalization. Patients are often reassured by the realization that someone will be with their family while they are separated by the surgery. When that person represents their God, their faith, and their community of faith, the support can be particularly helpful.

Discharge-Postdischarge

Early discharge is often a stressful event for patients. They may feel insecure in leaving the hospital before sufficient recovery. They may fear that they or their family cannot adequately cope once they are home. Discharge may require special arrangements for convalescent care at home such as home nursing care, therapies, or medical equipment.

Discharge may also mean a transfer to a rehabilitation program, convalescence center, or nursing care facility. Such a transfer may be temporary or permanent. Many older patients enter a nursing home upon discharge from the hospital. They may feel anxieties about coping, loss of independence, recovery, separation, and being a burden to family. These are serious adjustment issues at a time when many people are emotionally, physically, or intellectually impaired. It is a time when pastoral support and guidance may be very helpful.

There will always be unscheduled hospitalizations. The most common unscheduled admission is through the emergency room. This implies injury or a sudden onset of symptoms as in a heart attack. A physician who is treating an onset of symptoms or a crisis point in someone's disease may also counsel a quick admission for diagnostic purposes. Unexpected hospitalization often indicates a traumatic situation and calls for a ministry of crisis intervention.

In summary, the pressures on hospitals have initiated changes that significantly affect the way pastoral care is carried out in the hospital setting. People still look to their religious beliefs as the source of their values and to their pastors for guidance and support in such difficult times. Such choices are not merely cognitive, rational decisions but are rooted in a person's way of life and that which gives meaning. A crisis point calls out for personal care. Pastors who would bring the presence of Christ to their parishioners must do their homework as never before. Theological and ethical preparation must complement medical treatment if effective ministry is to take place. We look next at the forms of pastoral homework.

CHAPTER THREE

THE PASTOR'S HOMEWORK

ONE OF the questions heard most often from hospitalized patients is this one: Why is this happening to me? Occasionally, a patient has an answer already in mind and only seeks confirmation of that answer. "It's God's will. Everything has a purpose." Though this explanation for the problem of suffering appears theologically simple, it is probably the most commonly held explanation for a question that will be encountered again and again by pastors caring for their hospitalized parishioners. The pastor must be prepared to deal with the apparent conflict between the all-too-evident suffering in the world and belief in a God of infinite power and goodness whose will—at least on the surface—is assumed by many to be opposed to pain and evil. Other questions are equally compelling. What is the place of death in life? Is there really life after death? What about the pastor's own experience of mortality? These and other questions serve to point out the necessity of the pastor doing her homework long before entering the hospital to bring solace to the sick and dying. It is not crucial that the pastor have an answer for every occasion. There are instances of suffering that defy any attempt we might make to lend to them a measure of understanding. The pastor, however, should be able to help patients explore their own feelings about suffering and death.

That cannot be done effectively without adequate preparation in at least three areas: (1) the pastor confronting his own mortality, (2) the understanding of responses that have been made to the problem of suffering, and (3) the ability to help patients explore the meaning of, and move through, their own time of dying.

CONFRONTING OUR OWN MORTALITY

Throughout the course of his ministry, the pastor will be asked again and again to enter into the feelings of parishioners who are suffering and dying, help them to explore and understand those feelings, and then turn and walk away from their pain and mortality. Presence with parishioners and their families at the time of death is one of the most difficult ministries that the pastor is expected to perform. That task will be facilitated to the degree that the pastor has come to grips with his own suffering and death.

From the time that we are born, we are old enough to suffer and die, but there is little in our culture that encourages us to ponder or prepare for that eventuality. Just the opposite is true. From the time of childhood we are encouraged to deny death generally and our own death particularly. We avoid speaking the words. A physician brought word of a patient's death by saying to the patient's husband, "I'm sorry, but your wife did not survive the procedure." People do not survive the procedure; people "expire," like a warranty. They "pass away." A pastor spoke of a parishioner who "graduated into eternal life."

Such euphemisms are understandable. Suffering and death are frightening, but that fear must be conquered if we are to possess the ease, comfort, and sensitivity that are required to be with persons and their families meaningfully at such times in their lives.

Apart from the natural fear of what is painful and unknown, there are primarily two beliefs that serve to insulate us from pain and death. Psychiatrist Irvin D. Yalom wrote of the belief in "our own specialness." Limits, aging, death may apply to *them* but not to oneself, not to me. At a deep level one is convinced of one's personal invulnerability and imperishability.[1] We begin to learn this lesson as children. As parents, we would shield our children from life's unpleasantness. Children are encouraged to believe that when something goes wrong, Mom or Dad will fix it. It comes as a rude shock to discover that there are some things that our parents cannot mend. We rationalize not involving young children in the funerals of aged grandparents by a belief that "there is time enough for them to learn these things." We tend to teach our children that they are special, not subject to the same forces that rob adults of health and life.

A second belief that tends to insulate us from suffering and death derives from a truncated understanding of the Bible's teaching about misfortune. Having been written by many persons with different understandings and experiences of God's grace, the Bible presents a multifaceted teaching with regard to God's role in protecting believers from suffering and death. Such a varied witness serves to broaden and enrich our understanding, but it also allows us the freedom to pick and choose the understanding most congenial to us. Consequently, we tend to embrace Jesus' promise that "whatever you ask for in prayer with faith, you will receive" (Matthew 21:22), at the same time that we ignore Jesus' belief that God "makes his sun rise on the evil and on the good, and sends rain on the righteous and on the unrighteous" (Matthew 5:45). When the rain of a child's illness falls upon young parents, they may meet that crisis with heartfelt and persistent prayer, only to be forced to stand by, powerless to prevent their child's suffering and death. In the anger and pain of that kind of experience, it is not unusual to see people reject the God that they believed would watch over their child.

The Bible is full of [the] debate between what might be called the instinct of religion and the gospel of Christ. The natural instincts of religion demand that my life be given meaning by a special security against all of the insecurities of life. If it should seem as if goodness and evil—punishment for evil and reward for good—were not being properly correlated in life, then God will guarantee finally that they will be properly correlated.[2]

A better understanding of the gospel, however, would help us to recognize that "God's love would not be right if it were this kind of love. The Christian faith believes that within and beyond the tragedies and the contradictions of history we have laid hold upon a loving heart, the proof of whose love is first impartiality toward all of his children, and secondly a mercy which transcends good and evil."[3] The pastor's preparation for ministry in the presence of suffering and death begins at the point of confronting these truths. No one is exempt from pain and from death, not even the pastor. The feelings of powerlessness, futility, despair, and loneliness that come with the confrontation of suffering and death must be a part of the witness that the pastor brings to the sickroom. Henri Nouwen wrote pointedly that the pastor's "service will not be perceived as authentic unless it comes from a heart wounded by the suffering about which" he speaks.[4]

THE PROBLEM OF SUFFERING

Of all the issues that the pastor must confront, there is none that raises such a challenge to faith as the attempt to reconcile belief in a good and omnipotent God with "the problem of suffering, the mystery of iniquity, the strange and brutal haphazardness with which, as it seems at times, acute misfortune is distributed"[5] among persons. The issue was raised early in the history of the Christian church by the harsh persecution that the Romans imposed on the fledgling faith. Augustine confronted the question in his *Confessions*. Over the centuries since, theologians have attempted to provide explanation for the question in various ways. The pastor must be conversant with the most common approaches to this question if she is to help her parishioners interpret their own pain.[6] For example, the assumption that the experience of pain is part of God's will and that there is some purpose to be served by it is one of the more common interpretations advanced by hospitalized patients. The pastor may find this approach problematic; she may seek to help the person come to an explanation that she deems more theologically correct. In so doing, she may win the theological debate at the cost of not hearing a parishioner's underlying confusion as to what possible purpose could be served by his experience of pain. As a better approach, one might help the parishioner explore the difficulties involved in holding such a deterministic solution: Faithful patients commonly express the Pauline belief that God will not give them more pain than they are able to handle. In reality, some patients experience burdens of pain beyond any conceivable purpose or beyond their ability to cope. The more familiar a pastor is with approaches to the problem of pain, the better able she will be to enter her parishioner's world of pain and bring healing. We examine here seven approaches to the problem.

One approach, similar to the one we have been examining, accepts suffering as a mystery that must necessarily be borne in the course of living. There are many, however, who find it impossible to hold such a position. There are instances of suffering, such as the Holocaust, that seem to defy any possible purpose on God's part. Some persons might react by saying that "if my suffering is God's will, then I want nothing to do with God." As an all-embracing explanation, the approach fails at the point of its inability to explain evil that is clearly the result of other agencies, such as human freedom.

A second popular explanation is that which attributes evil, pain, and suffering to a dualistic source. By positing the existence of an evil being or force, such as Satan, it is possible to attribute all evil to an evil "god," thereby absolving the God of our faith. The approach is very popular in our generation, which is enamored with the demonic and has explored it to a great degree in popular film and literary genre. The explanation, however, runs afoul of God's omnipotence. "Why," some have asked, "would a good God tolerate the evil brought about by a spirit contrary to his?" While the explanation allows us the luxury of explaining all evil through the agency of a source outside ourselves, it also fails to hold us accountable for our own actions, actions that quite clearly bring a high degree of suffering upon many people. If it is said that God will triumph over Satan in the end, that provides small solace for those suffering intensely now. They may well regard such solace as "pie in the sky, by and by."

A third explanation, if not speaking to the question of the origin of the problem of pain, nevertheless finds pain and evil to serve the purpose of helping to highlight their opposites. The awareness of the nature of evil and suffering becomes a factor in the value we place upon health and goodness. The cold grayness of a dreary day serves to heighten our appreciation of a warm sunny day. The awareness of what a dreaded disease such as cancer can do to the body leads us to be grateful for the health that we have. It might even be said by some that we might be unable to appreciate life at all if it were not for the presence of death. There is an element of truth in this approach. Certainly, we celebrate the appearance of the sun all that much more after having been confined to the house by a blizzard. There are, however, instances of evil and suffering that are so great as to defy any possible appreciation of goodness. There are those who, far from being brought to a heightened awareness of goodness, are instead led to reject the God who appears to allow such massive amounts of evil as can be found in the Holocaust and Vietnam. If a drought serves to help us appreciate a drenching thunderstorm, what of those whose crops fail and whose farms are taken from them as a result of the drought?

A fourth, widely held explanation for the presence of suffering in the world, finds it to be the means by which God punishes people for their sin. Growing out of an Old Testament legal code, which required "an eye for an eye," the interpretation was widespread in Jesus' time and has persisted, particularly among Christianity's more conservative interpreters. It is an interpretation that is often found in persons who experience suffering and death in connection with an event that they perceive as having violated God's will. For example, young couples whose ardor leads to a pregnancy out-of-wedlock may feel that God is punishing them if the baby subsequently dies. There are those who would explain the AIDS epidemic that stalks our planet as God's punishment of those who share a different life-style or who use drugs.

There are a number of stumbling blocks in this approach. For as many as believe that God has ordained suffering to punish people for sin, there are equally as many more who find such a God to be sadistic and reject him outright. It is difficult to account for natural forces that bring suffering, such as tornadoes or famine, by resorting to this approach. When famine in poorer nations causes thousands of persons to die of starvation, it does not make sense to assume that all of these people were sinners who deserved such a fate. While the death of a child may be seen as punishment for its erring parents, what of the child itself? In what measure can the child be considered to be so sinful as to merit death?

In spite of these problems, however, the interpretation remains popular. Dorothee Soelle, though not an advocate of the approach herself, finds such a belief at work in some who are reluctant to work with suffering people or to go to funeral homes.[7]

A fifth approach to explaining the origin of suffering, an interpretation whose appeal is increased by its plausibility, finds most suffering to be the result of misuse of the freedom that God gave to us. Freedom is the essential prerequisite to the worth of any decision to follow God's leading. If we are not free to reject God's lead, then the decision to live according to what we perceive to be God's will amounts to little more than the knee-jerk reaction of a marionette. But freedom is a perilous gift. Many use their freedom to live in a moral manner; many others choose to use their freedom to hurt and exploit other people. One person may use freedom to participate in creation, investing a life in research to discover a cure for a painful disease. Another may use freedom to sexually abuse little children.

It is that very freedom itself that raises the first objection to the approach. Why, some might ask, did God give us so much freedom that we are able to cause such incredible pain? Couldn't we have survived with a little less freedom? "Why must there be so much liberty that some individuals can become thoroughly depraved?"[8] Some might feel that the high degree of freedom given to us makes God responsible for much of the evil and pain in the world. Nor can natural disasters, such as earthquake and flood, be easily accounted for under this scheme of things.

A sixth approach to the problem of suffering finds pain to be a means by which God tests the strength of our devotion to him. God's testing of Abraham in Genesis 22 became the means by which God became assured of Abraham's love and loyalty.

Suffering brought about in such a way can become the means by which God teaches lessons of discipline that help to forge a durable faith. "No pain, no gain," say some athletes, who find injury to be the means by which they become stronger and more resistant to pain.

There is a measure of truth to this approach. Certainly, it is the pain of "hitting bottom" that provides the means for many an alcoholic to admit powerlessness over the disease and turn her life over to God for healing. In moments of extreme suffering, persons find a determination and courage that they never dreamed they possessed. On the other hand, for those who find the story of Abraham's test appealing, there are also those who feel that a God who would put a father through such an ordeal is not worthy of our devotion. Such a God may well be seen as insensitive and uncaring. One might wonder what sort of lesson is to be learned through events of mass destruction. When a tornado kills innocent children, it is difficult to account for that event in terms of any testing or lesson to be learned.

A final approach to the problem of suffering can be built out of an understanding that sees the universe not as a finished product, but rather as a product in process of completion and in whose incompleteness is contained forces that act against the good purposes of the Creator.[9] Such an approach, though built on a more limited understanding of God's omnipotence, nevertheless removes the dilemma created by belief in a God who has all the power to remove suffering and appears to be unwilling to do so. In the unfinished creation, we are given freedom to become co-creators with God in the challenging task of bringing order to the chaos. Though we may experience pain as a result of our freedom, the option to work with God in the humanizing of the creation lends meaning and stability to our existence. In such a universe, God does not sit far off, like some "unmoved Mover," but rather becomes vulnerable to rejection. God knows that "to love is to be vulnerable—vulnerable to the hurts and risks that come from setting the other free and accepting his freedom."[10] As for natural disasters, they may be seen as part of the forces at work in an incomplete creation that is "groaning in travail" (Romans

8:22). If God is vulnerable, then it is a vulnerability in which God stands with us in our suffering and shares our pain. If such a limiting of God's power seems to render God weak, the approach is fully in keeping with the God of Jesus Christ whose "power is made perfect in weakness" (II Corinthians 12:9). It is in the very cross of Christ that God fully shared pain and death as we know it and yet brought about an end to both through his gift of eternal life.

THE REALITY OF DEATH

Pastors who would bring comfort to hospitalized patients must have confronted the reality of their own eventual death. If they have not, much that they say will appear shallow and meaningless. A patient asked his physician, "Am I going to die?" His physician replied, "We're *all* going to die sometime." The physician's answer, while certainly true, ducked the issue. The patient persisted, "Yes, I know, but am *I* going to die from the illness that I have now?" Unwilling to confront the issue, his doctor answered, "I don't know."

Denial in the face of death is common in our culture and has been well-documented.[11] Moreover, the physician noted above did expect his patient to die and rationalized his answer by saying that "only God knows when someone will die." But that answer is also partial truth. Many patients believe that they are going to die. They merely seek confirmation from their physician of what they already suspect. Somewhat later in the morning, I received a telephone page by the patient's nurse, who told me that the physician had entered an order in the patient's chart for pastoral care—for a visit to the patient because "he wanted to talk about dying." The patient asked me the same question: "Am I going to die?" I answered, "Yes, it's very possible." The answer led to a long and meaningful conversation with the patient about his life and its meaning and what plans he felt he had to make now that it might end.

Like the physician just noted, pastors may be uncomfortable when talking about death. The feelings that accompany death-awareness are not necessarily pleasant. We are social beings by nature; we enjoy the company of family and friends. Death, on the other hand, reminds us that there is a basic aloneness to life. We die alone; no one can go with us on that journey. We will leave the most beloved of family members behind, and the loneliness may be intense from that awareness.

A sense of powerlessness and futility comes with the knowledge that you are going to die. The feeling is exacerbated in a culture that relies upon human cleverness and intellect. "If it isn't broken, don't fix it." Death reminds us that there is nothing that we can do to "fix" it. It will have its way with us no matter what we feel or do.

There is a sense of having been rudely brought back to earth with a painful bump. We recognize that we are no more special than anyone else. People are born; people die. Life goes on without a blink. Someone, speaking of his own death, once said, "I always thought that in my case an exception would be made." An awareness of death contains the realization that there are no exceptions. No matter how well we've lived, no matter how faithfully, we are of the "dust, and to dust" we shall return (Genesis 3:19).

Death brings with it the fear that we feel when facing the unknown. Even pastors who have stood by the bedside of many persons at the time of their death have no knowledge of what their own death will be like. There is a stark physicality to dying. At the time of death, persons' eyes are frequently wide open, staring sightlessly into space. A person's mouth may be agape, as if struggling for one last breath. Depending on the disease that claimed the person, the room may be filled with unpleasant odors; the patient's appearance may not be pleasant; his last minutes may be such as to make others hope that "I never die that way." What cosmetics creates in the funeral home is a far cry from death's actual appearance. Some people, upon witnessing the death of someone they love, avoid hospitals forever after, robbing those they love of even the gift of their presence. Apart from nursing staff, the pastor is the only professional person who is called to share the last moments of life with parishioners.

Awareness begins by experiencing the emotions already noted.

It is facilitated by recognizing that death is a natural part of life. Author Annie Dillard discovered it in the natural world around her and noted that there is "a covenant to which every thing, every hydrogen atom, is bound. The terms are clear: if you want to live, you have to die."[12] Ecclesiastes tells us that there is "a time to be born, and a time to die" (3:2).

To all of the emotions created by death, we bring the powerful sustenance of faith. In the face of the aloneness and isolation of life's last journey, we know that even in "the valley of the shadow of death" we need "fear no evil," for God has promised to walk "with me" (Psalm 23:4). To all of the powerlessness is brought the knowledge that Christ triumphed over death and that God's "power is made perfect in weakness" (II Corinthians 12:9). If it seems that our lives have been robbed of their specialness by death's reality, then the Bible reminds us also that we have been created only a "little less than God" (Psalm 8:5); so important to our Creator are we that the hairs of our heads "are all numbered" (Luke 12:7). The fear of that which is unknown is more than eased in knowing into whose hands it is that we commit our spirits (Luke 23:46).

There is a sense in which it can be said that we experience death every day. Elisabeth Kübler-Ross reminds us that dying

is something we human beings do continuously, not just at the end of our physical lives on this earth. The stages of dying . . . apply . . . to any significant change (e.g., retirement, moving to a new city, changing jobs, divorce) in a person's life, and change is a regular occurrence in human existence. If you can face and understand your ultimate death, perhaps you can learn to face and deal productively with each change that presents itself in your life. . . . And through a lifetime of such commitment, you can face your final end with peace and joy, knowing that you have lived your life well.[13]

When we are able to face the impact of death and our own inclusion in it, then we can even be freed by that awareness to envision our lives in a new and more meaningful way. The awareness of death reminds us of the value of life. In my work as a hospital chaplain, I am constantly with patients whose confrontation with death has caused them to evaluate and rearrange their priorities. When you know that a day may be your last, it becomes imperative to see each day as a gift of God's creating to be lived to the fullest. Irvin Yalom reminds us that "death and life are interdependent: though the physicality of death destroys us, the *idea* of death saves us. Recognition of death contributes a sense of poignancy to life, provides a radical shift of life perspective, and can transport one from a mode of living characterized by diversions, tranquilization, and petty anxieties to a more authentic mode."[14] The acceptance of death leads us to the celebration of life, to the desire to live each day to the fullest, and to approach life's ending with a confident faith in God's ability to give us life eternal. Out of such an experience the pastor is enabled to bring special gifts to those who are dying.

One of those gifts is a changed orientation to death. It is common to envision death as something that happens to us. While that is true, it is also possible to approach death as something that we do. Having celebrated our lives to the fullest, death can be seen as that act in which we faithfully accept God's promise of new life in Christ, and give our lives over to God's keeping. I have been called out of bed in the middle of the night to be with a dying patient who asked for prayer and who died immediately after prayer was given. I am convinced that people are able to summon up just enough life to enable an act of faith to be performed before death. In a very real way, they have taken to heart Jesus' conviction regarding his life that "no one takes it from me, but I lay it down of my own accord . . . this charge I have received from my Father" (John 10:18).

Another gift is that of caring presence. Although death's journey must of necessity be made alone, we can be with persons in the moment leading up to that transition. A dying student nurse asked movingly for just such a gift.

I know you feel insecure, don't know what to say, don't know what to do. But please believe me, if you care, you can't go wrong. Just admit that you care. That is really for what we search. We may ask for why's and wherefore's, but we don't really expect answers. Don't run away—wait—all I want to know is that there will be someone to hold my hand when I need it. I am afraid. Death may get to be a routine to you, but it is new to me. You may not see me as unique, but I've never died before. To me, once is pretty unique![15]

Finally, in the moments after death there is given to the pastor a unique opportunity to offer commendatory prayer for the deceased. The prayer may express thanksgiving for the life of the deceased and the good memories that remain; it may raise questions that prey on the minds of the family members present; it may offer their grief to God with a plea for the comfort and strength to pick up the pieces of their lives and faithfully go on. When appropriate, I like to include words of thanks for the nurses and physicians who gave of their God-given talents to bring comfort. When that is done, it is not unusual for a nurse to express her own "Thanks!" for being included among those whose lives were touched by the deceased.

Death touches all of us. In confronting its reality and coming to terms with her own death, the pastor is given opportunity to transform a time of dying into a celebrative thanksgiving for life itself. There is no substitute for doing the homework that enables hospital ministry to take place.

CHAPTER FOUR

THE PASTOR'S BIO-ETHICS

THE ADVANCEMENT of medical-scientific research over the last twenty years has been astonishing. Its discoveries have enabled researchers to step into worlds that our ancestors never dreamed would be explored. The discovery of DNA, the basic building block of genes, has led researchers to speculate about coming into contact with the elements of life itself. New discoveries in the area of gene therapy have raised the possibility of creating people on a made-to-order basis. Research into the elements that make up viruses has elevated hope that cures may be found for some of the most dreaded diseases to which humans are subject.

Along with the fruit of research has come a growing concern that our scientific capability may outstrip our ability to think theologically about and ethically manage our achievements. The hospital, particularly the large teaching hospital, has become one of the primary focal points for the exploration and application of the medical-ethical issues raised by our achievements.

For pastors, the issues raise questions about the very essence of life and death. Jesus said, "I came that [you] may have life, and have it abundantly" (John 10:10). But what is the nature of the life that he brought? Can it be said that a fertilized egg in a test tube constitutes life? Does a person existing in a persistently vegetative state (PVS) have life? What of the gravely ill patient whose electroencephalograms (EEG) have indicated the absence of any electrical activity in the brain? In what sense can such a patient be said to have "life"? Increasingly, pastors are being asked to journey with parishioners through issues of just such complexity. For the most part, these issues tend to crystallize in decisions that are faced at the beginning and at the ending of life.

ISSUES AT LIFE'S INCEPTION

Does life ever take a more miraculous form than at birth? The birth of a child is the fulfillment of our dreams for becoming co-creators of life with God, and for the extension of our lives beyond our earthly time. Few moments are more filled with joy and meaning than that of birth. As fraught with promise as childbirth is, however, it may also become the time in which persons are confronted with some of the most agonizing decisions they will ever have to make. Two areas require exploration: embryo transplantation and abortion.

Physicians now have the ability to extract eggs from a woman, place them in a petri dish, fertilize them with sperm, and replace them in a woman's uterus in the hope of implantation and the eventual birth of a child. This has brought tremendous hope to infertile couples who have repeatedly tried to give birth to children without success. The process has also created a number of dilemmas and questions. For example, does having the ability to give a viable embryo to a previously infertile woman mean that all women should now be able to bear children? What of women who do not wish to marry but desire to have a child? Should childbearing be separated from the marital relationship? Put differently, should the creative act be separated from the expression of love? The use of surrogate mothers has created other problems. The news media have carried the stories of surrogate mothers who, after carrying a child through the period of gestation, are unable at birth to give up the child to the parents who paid for the service. Who is the real mother of the child?

Two other issues are particularly troublesome. With in vitro fertilization (IVF) has come the possibility of selecting the sex, abilities, and personality characteristics that parents would like to have in their child. They can "order" the kind of child that they want. At that point we have moved far afield from overcoming infertility. Who decides what "kinds" of persons are "best"? Should anyone be entitled to make such a choice?

Of even greater concern to some is the matter of ova loss. Because successful implantation of an embryo is a process that requires repeated attempts, several ova are required. These eggs, produced through hormonal stimulation of the ovaries, are then fertilized with sperm. Once cell division has taken place, the embryo is inserted into the uterus. Upon successful implantation, what happens to the other frozen embryos? Do these embryos constitute mini-human life? Can they be discarded? Does discarding them constitute an abortion? And, to whom do the other frozen embryos belong after pregnancy has taken place?

Just as embryo transplantation raises questions at the creation of life, abortion raises questions of a particularly agonizing nature when a decision is made to terminate life. I remember being called one morning to the bedside of a young woman who was scheduled to abort her pregnancy. Because of an illness contracted at the beginning of her pregnancy, before she knew that she was pregnant, she had taken a drug prescribed for her that was known to have disastrous effects upon an unborn child. When she later found out that she was expecting a baby, she faced the dilemma of giving birth to a seriously deformed infant. Amid great soul searching, she elected to terminate the pregnancy. A strong Roman Catholic, her up-bringing had taught her that, apart from its being done to save her own life, abortion was morally wrong in all cases. Now, on the eve of the termination, she tearfully talked with me about her decision and the despair and guilt that filled that decision with pain.

There are primarily three positions in the discussion about the ethics of abortion. The conservative position states that abortion is virtually never acceptable and, if considered, may only be considered for the purpose of saving the life of the mother. A liberal position holds that abortion is a matter existing between a mother and her physician and that a woman has an inherent right to make her own decisions on matters affecting her own body. A somewhat middle-of-the-road position holds that abortion is permissible up to a certain stage of fetal development, given a certain set of mitigating physical or moral circumstances. Such circumstances may be the means by which the pregnancy took place, for example by rape or incest; the question of the emotional or physical life of the mother; the judgment of the quality of life that may be expected for the fetus.

Central to any decision to terminate a pregnancy is a crucial question: When does human life begin? Opinions on the question range all the way from the feeling that human life begins at the moment of fertilization to that of the moment of birth itself. Between those two extremes are those who argue that the moment in which a mother is first able to feel fetal movement is the point at which life begins; still others hold that life exists only at the point at which a fetus is able to survive outside the uterus.

There are at least three ethical issues that must be considered in any decision to terminate a pregnancy. The first of these has to do with the ontological status of the fetus. Put plainly, what sort of being is the fetus? Is the fetus a human being? If it is, what sort of "human-ness" does it possess? "Human" may refer to the setting of the genetic code that distinguishes us from the other animals. It can also refer to life that is distinctively human. For example, humans are thought to be the only animals that are aware of and spend time thinking about the fact that they will eventually die. On a more positive note, to be human can be said to be indicative of one's ability to make rational decisions, to communicate in symbols, or to commit oneself to a life of loving another particular person.

This issue becomes particularly important when we consider the matter of terminating a pregnancy that has entered its second trimester. Such terminations are usually justified, among other reasons, on the basis of the quality of human life that the fetus can be expected to enjoy after birth. When, through ultra-sound imaging or amniocentesis, it is learned that a fetal anomaly exists, terminations of such fetuses are often justified on their possessing an anomaly that is believed to be incompatible with human life.

The question of quality of life can be seen in several ways. A fetus may be born with a condition known to cause death within a matter of hours or days. The infant may live briefly, but at what quality? A fetus may be born with a condition that is believed to be fatal within a period of weeks or months, during which time that infant may need constant medical care just to survive to its time of dying. Can such a life be called human? The pastor must help the patient decide.

Upon maintaining that the fetus is a person, the issues are complicated still further. How do we define personhood? If the possession of a genetic structure is sufficient for personhood, then clearly the fetus qualifies. If, however, the ability to communicate with other persons in a language understandable to both of them is the criteria, then it would seem that the fetus does not qualify. The issue of ontology is very complex.

The second ethical issue has to do with the moral status of the fetus. Put differently, at what point does the fetus possess a moral right to protection? In the well-known 1973 *Roe* vs. *Wade* decision, the United States Supreme Court decided that, prior to viability, the fetus enjoyed no legal rights. The question of moral rights was not addressed by the Court and remains one of the ethical foci of persons holding a religious faith.

In the Judeo-Christian tradition, the earliest mention of artificially induced termination of pregnancy is found in the law code of Exodus 21:22-25. The passage deals with the accidental death of a fetus through injury done to the mother. In this case, the perpetrator of the act is obligated to pay a fine to the husband of the injured wife, but no penalty is exacted for the death of the fetus. Only in the event of the mother's death does the law of "an eye for an eye" apply. It seems clear that the fetus has no moral status. There are other biblical passages that have to do with the act of committing murder, but they do not appear to have been intended to deal specifically with the act of abortion. Nor does the New Testament speak specifically of the act.

The Christian church has taken several different positions over the last twenty centuries. Exploration of those positions would take us beyond our purpose of highlighting the issues involved in medical-ethical decision-making. Today the issue is joined by conservative folk who feel that the unborn fetus has full moral status and those of a more liberal persuasion who feel that the fetus has no more rights than a tumor, or any other piece of tissue, and which, like the tumor, may be cut out and disposed of. In between are many moderates who hold that the fetus has partial moral rights, usually linked to what is seen to be the point at which the fetus is able to survive on its own outside the uterus.

The third ethical issue has to do with rights. Whose rights are more important: those of the fetus or those of the mother? Albert Outler summed up the problem concisely by noting that "in the decision for or against abortion, what is being weighed is the life of the fetus against the anguish of the mother, and these incommensurables create a profound moral dilemma."[1]

The issue may run even deeper than that. What may be faced is making a choice between one life or the other. If one holds a position that both the fetus and the mother have rights, then whose rights prevail when it is clear that one cannot live without the death of the other?

A conservative approach to this issue may embrace the life of the fetus over that of the mother. A liberal approach holds the mother's life in esteem. The moderate attempts to pick her way through the problems of both positions to come to an option that will satisfy more people by according rights to the fetus at a particular point in time, usually that of viability. Having done that, however, the moderate must then decide *which* rights decide and in *what* cases termination may take place. Is rape a sufficient cause to choose the rights of the mother over those of the fetus? If the life of the mother is the basis that is chosen, does that include the emotional life of the mother (the basis for what is usually called "therapeutic" abortion)?

Clearly, the issues involved in the termination of pregnancy are of a deep, wrenching, painful nature. My own faith tradition notes that such a decision should be made "only after thoughtful and prayerful consideration by the parties involved, with medical, pastoral, and other appropriate counsel."[2] Even after prayer and counsel, a decision to terminate a pregnancy may scar people for life.

ISSUES AT LIFE'S ENDING

With the development of medical technology has also come the ability to support and extend life dramatically. With that extension has arisen a host of ethical questions related to the level of medical care that should be extended to patients who may be nearing the end of their lives.

There are primarily four levels of medical care familiar to most of us: (1) general medical and surgical care extended to persons who come into their physician's office or hospital with illnesses that can be treated and reversed, (2) emergency resuscitation, provided to patients who experience a sudden life-threatening emergency such as heart attack or drowning, (3) intensive care and advanced life support, which may be provided to critically ill patients, some of whom may have doubtful prognosis, and (4) general nursing and physician care, such as is found in a hospice, aimed at keeping a patient comfortable, usually with the expectation that the patient will die within the near future. The first category raises no questions in our minds; we expect such basic medical care to be available to all persons. Questions begin to arise with the provision of emergency resuscitation and advanced life support, particularly when such care is extended to patients whose prognosis is poor and whose quality of life upon survival appears questionable. At this point, we begin to consider three issues that relate to the Christian's respect for the sanctity of life as it has been created by God.

Code Status

Code status is the term most commonly used to designate whether or not a patient should receive emergency resuscitation upon experiencing a respiratory or cardiac arrest while in the hospital. Patients are commonly classified as "full code," indicating that all resuscitative measures should be undertaken to preserve their life, or as "no code," indicating that, upon experiencing a respiratory or cardiac emergency, they should be allowed to die without receiving treatment that could delay or reverse their death. Pastors may well be asked by families to take part in case conferences in which patients or families are asked to make such a decision for themselves or for a loved one.

Whenever possible, such a decision should be made by the patient concerned. The issue at this point is whether or not the patient is competent to make such a decision. There are generally three principles by which competence is determined.

First, the patient must have the ability to reason and to make judgments. Second, the decision to ask for or to forgo emergency resuscitative treatment must be made voluntarily and without coercion. Third, the patient must have a clear understanding of the risks and benefits of the proposed treatment alternatives or nontreatment, along with a full understanding of the nature of the disease and the prognosis.[3] When a patient, whose body is riddled by a painful metastatic cancer, makes a decision not to be resuscitated in an emergency, such a decision may be difficult for her family to accept. The pastor's ability to sensitively help family members focus on the quality of that patient's life coupled with the assurance of God's continuing care for them and for the patient may serve to help such a decision be made. However, when the patient is relatively young, suffers from an illness that can be reversed, and can anticipate good quality of life, the decision becomes much more difficult. I remember warmly an active woman, recently retired, who made just such a decision to the dismay of her family and friends. She made her choice not to undergo life-sustaining treatment preeminently out of her sense of satisfaction at a life long and well lived, as well as not wanting to spend her remaining days in a nursing care institution in which she felt that she would be a burden to those who cared for her.

Where it is judged that patients are not competent to make a decision for or against emergency resuscitation, it usually falls to their family members to make that decision for them. This can be an extremely difficult decision for them to make. It may be complicated by prior experiences, religious beliefs, or broken relationships. Physicians prefer a sense of unanimity among family members when making a no-code decision. Occasionally, there may be one family member who, perhaps out of a sense of guilt, may not be willing to join with other family members in allowing a parent to die. The pastor may be able to help that person explore the feelings that cause him to stand in the way of the family's making a decision.

Most people whose lives are lived primarily outside a hospital setting do not realize what takes place when a "Code Blue" is called for a patient. They have seen numerous medical programs on television in which a code is called, the code team responds, and the patient is rescued from the danger of imminent death. Reality is quite different. Most attempts at cardiopulmonary resuscitation are futile. The success rate may be as low as 10 percent.[4] The procedure itself is quite violent. Chest compressions, if done properly in place of an arrested heartbeat, may fracture ribs. Patients who experience electrical defibrillation as part of a particular cardiac therapy describe it as very unpleasant. Powerful drugs are given that may have unanticipated harmful side effects on a person. Family members need to be more aware of these facts than they commonly are, particularly in cases in which their loved one cannot reasonably expect good quality of life upon survival.

Most code decisions come in the form of deciding either to resuscitate or to allow a patient to die naturally. Occasionally, a decision is made to allow some, but not all, resuscitative measures. These decisions are frequently problematic for hospital staff, who are told that they can do some things but not everything within their power to restore a patient. Such decisions are called "chemical codes" (only drugs are administered) or "partial codes" and may be suggested by a physician only to make a family feel that everything possible is being done for their loved one, particularly when a family is opposed to making a no-code decision. Patients may receive a "Do not Intubate" status, which prohibits the placement of a breathing tube into their airway. This may be done in cases in which it is feared that, once a patient is placed on a ventilator, she may become ventilator-dependent, unable to be weaned off the ventilator. This is particularly a danger for patients with chronic respiratory problems. When a patient is placed upon therapies such as mechanical ventilation (commonly called a breathing machine) and high dosage of powerful intravenous drugs, we have then moved into an area in which the ethical dilemmas raised by the life-support treatment are much more complex.

The Withdrawal of Support

When we discuss the removal of life support from a patient, we are simultaneously talking about the patient's death. Our dilemma is that "along with our enhanced technologic power we don't seem to have better judgment; with increasing ability to be invasive we aren't more gentle; with dramatic power to work with life we don't have a better understanding about the nature of life itself. If today's doctors can 'prevent' the immediacy of death, if our technology can temporarily delay death, then someone must decide wisely on the due season for death. In the midst of tubes, lines, and powerful pressor drugs, when shall we die?"[5]

This question became very concrete when "Ben" entered the hospital. He underwent coronary artery bypass surgery and "coded" on the operating room table. Through the insertion of an intra-aortic balloon pump, a device that assists the heart's pumping action, Ben was kept alive and arrived in the surgical intensive care unit. Within hours he coded again and CPR successfully restored his heartbeat. Gradually, however, Ben's condition continued to deteriorate. Powerful intravenous drugs were given to maintain his blood pressure; the ventilator kept him breathing, but his kidneys shut down and he did not awaken. The machinery and drugs kept Ben alive for the better part of a week, but it became increasingly apparent that Ben would not survive. Eventually, a conference was scheduled with Ben's family to discuss disconnecting the machinery that was keeping Ben alive. Ben's wife asked that their pastor be present at the conference.

Such conferences are common in hospital care today, and they raise a number of ethical concerns. When life support is withdrawn from a patient, are we in effect killing that patient? What gives us the right to decide when a patient should die; isn't that God's responsibility? How do we know that it is the right time to turn off the machinery? If we wait a few days to make the decision, might not the patient suddenly recover his strength and survive? For families caught in the midst of these kinds of situations, such a decision can be the most heart-wrenching experience they have ever had.

We are describing "extraordinary" means of life support. There are some who feel that the terms *ordinary* and *extraordinary* may not be most helpful. A recent publication by the Hastings Center suggests abandoning these terms in favor of *burdens* and *benefits*, noting that "all treatments that impose undue burdens on the patient without overriding benefits or that simply provide no benefits may justifiably be withheld or withdrawn."[6]

When a patient is comatose and examination indicates that there is no longer any electrical activity present in her brain to enable her to sustain life, a decision to remove support, while painful, may seem understandable. However, when a patient lapses into a persistent vegetative state, the matter becomes even more complex. For many who follow these matters, the names of Karen Ann Quinlan and Nancy Cruzan come immediately to mind. Both cases were widely reported in the news media. Following catastrophic injury, both women lapsed into what is called a persistent vegetative state (PVS), which lasted for years, during which time their parents struggled in the court system to have them removed from life support and allowed to die. A noted neurologist has distinguished a persistent vegetative state from a coma by noting that "in a coma the patient's eyes are closed, but in a persistent vegetative state the patient is awake but unaware, has sleep-wake cycles, but is unconscious and unable to interact purposefully with [the] environment. There is virtually no chance that such a patient will ever recover consciousness."[7] Patients who exist in such a state are kept alive by artificial nutrition and hydration, food and water administered through various tubes implanted in them. It is one thing to discuss disconnecting a ventilator, forcing a critically ill patient to assume the responsibility of breathing for himself. Some patients successfully do so and go on to recover. For patients who live in a PVS, however, the removal of nutrition and hydration means certain death and raises the specter of euthanasia in the minds of some. There are volumes available which explore all of these subjects in a depth not possible for this treatment.[8] A number of issues are relevant for pastoral care, however, and need to be examined.

First, the removal of life support does not mean that we are deliberately killing a patient. Our medical technology has advanced to the degree that we can thwart death almost indefinitely. Removing a ventilator or dialysis machine from a hopelessly ill patient may mean only that the patient is being afforded the opportunity to live or die as he would, had medicine not intervened. That the machinery is available does not mean that in every case it must be used. There is a dignity to dying naturally, which many patients choose. When, because of their condition, they are unable to make such a decision, it becomes a gift that family members can give to them.

Second, a patient's choice to forgo life-sustaining treatment is not an indication of lack of competence. Pastors are familiar with the patient who has enjoyed a full and meaningful life, who believes that God holds greater meaning and love for her beyond death, and who does not want to continue to live in a manner that seems devoid of fulfillment or as a burden to those who love her. A person has the right to make that choice. It is part of the freedom God gives us and within which we choose to follow God's leading.

Third, any suggested medical treatment, including a proposal to withdraw support, should follow the principles of burden and benefit. If treatment will ultimately benefit a patient by extending meaningful life as defined by that patient and her family, let it be pursued. There are numerous studies, however, that suggest that the provision of artificial nutrition and hydration to patients who are terminally ill may *not* be of benefit to them. "Patients who are allowed to die without artificial hydration and nutrition may well die more comfortably than patients who receive conventional amounts of intravenous hydration. Terminal pulmonary edema, nausea, and mental confusion are more likely when patients have been treated to maintain fluid and nutrition until close to the time of death.''[9] Issues such as these are among the most emotionally painful choices that persons are ever called on to make. They are frequently made in the absence of clear-cut absolute principles that would seem to mandate one course of action over another. It is held here, however, that there do exist four general guidelines that can be of help in making any decisions regarding life support.

First, there must be a great amount of certainty on the part of the physician that an incompetent patient's condition will not improve significantly. Pastors can be of help in facilitating communication between the physician and family members at this point. People are often reticent to question physicians or to press them for further information in the face of a proposed course of treatment that they do not understand. Unfortunately, when dealing with a patient who is dying, physicians are not always careful to take the time necessary to interpret treatment modalities or care for the feelings experienced by patients and family members who are facing death. The pastor can be an advocate for the patient and his family, helping to ensure that the time is taken to leave persons feeling as good as possible about the choices that they must make.

Second, utmost care must be taken to preserve the comfort of patients who are dying. Cancer patients who are in the last stage of their illness are often placed on an intravenous morphine drip to help control the pain that may go with cancer. Similarly, when considering the removal of life-support equipment, the guiding principle should be the comfort of the patient. If removing support will increase a patient's pain, then it should not be removed.

Third, physicians should make it clear that the removal of life support does not mean that the patient is being abandoned. In the face of death there exists in the minds of many patients a deep fear of separation. Patients need to know that they will not be left alone.

Finally, every effort should be made to abide by the patient's own wishes with regard to treatment. Many, perhaps most, states now have legislation that allows people to state their wishes with regard to life support. Two vehicles exist for this purpose. The Living Will enables patients to stipulate that, in the event their physician determines that they have a terminal illness in which death is imminent, they do not wish to have their lives prolonged by extraordinary means of life support; it also states their desire to be allowed to die in as pain-free a condition as possible. The value of the Living Will is limited. It depends on the physician's determination that a patient's illness is not treatable. There are physicians who are reluctant to give up treatment. It must be drafted by the patient at a time when there is no question about the patient's competence. A better choice is the Durable Power of Attorney for Health Care (DPA). This instrument, executed by a competent person, designates an agent to make health care decisions for the patient in the event that the patient is not competent to act on her own behalf. Commonly, the DPA also allows a patient to stipulate the removal of artificial nutrition and hydration. It does not depend on a physician's determination as to whether an illness is treatable or not. The 1991 Patient Determination Act mandates that all hospitals and health care facilities inform patients upon admission of their right to refuse medical treatment. Unfortunately, by the time a patient is admitted to the hospital or nursing home, it may be too late to make such a decision. A patient may no longer be competent. There is a real role to be played at this point by pastors. Pastors can include information about these choices in sermons and newsletters; study groups provide an excellent setting for distributing the instruments and helping people to draft them at a time when they are not under the pressure of illness. It has been my experience that many persons, particularly those who are elderly, have a great sense of relief after making arrangements ahead of time. Many persons anticipate that, in the not-too-distant future, most of us will die managed deaths. That raises a final consideration.

Euthanasia

Behind all that we have been saying, there is the question of euthanasia. When we give assent to a plea from a loved one for the removal of life support, do we become guilty of killing that person or tacitly assisting that person in his own suicide? There are some who feel that "the pleas of the very seriously ill as they beg at times to be put to death are hardly to be understood as conveying a real desire for euthanasia.''[10] Still others wonder, ''Why do we treat our aged and loved animals better than we treat our aged and loved human beings?''[11]

Euthanasia is understood as actively taking the life of another person, or passively assisting a person in taking his own life. Those who oppose euthanasia feel that removing life support from a terminally ill patient disregards the sanctity of human life and takes from God the judgment as to when to end a life. They believe that such a choice violates the commandment against killing and feel that, if euthanasia is sanctioned, it will open the door to ''pulling the plug'' on any person or class of persons judged to have questionable quality of life. In contrast, euthanasia's supporters believe that everyone has the right to die in dignity at a time and manner of personal choosing in the event of a painful and dehumanizing terminal illness. Best known among proponents of euthanasia is the National Hemlock Society.[12] The issue is complex and continues to evolve. That these issues are far from easily decided is testimony to the value of God's gift of life.

CHAPTER FIVE

FINDING YOUR WAY IN THE HOSPITAL

WHEN MOSES sent spies into the promised land, the spies returned with the report that the land was well fortified and occupied by giants. "All the people that we saw in it are of great size . . . and to ourselves we seemed like grasshoppers, and so we seemed to them" (Numbers 13:32-33).

Many pastors experience a similar feeling when they visit a parishioner in the hospital. If they do not find the hospital intimidating, it is often bewildering. The hospital is a complex organization with a physical plant that may be a confusing labyrinth of rooms and corridors. At one time hospitals were clearly structured, and the personnel wore uniforms that clearly identified who they were. Now you can enter a hospital and never see a nurse's cap. The only specific identification might be an "R.N." on her (or his) nametag. There is a confusing array of titles, degrees, and functions, making it difficult to distinguish between nurse, therapist (of different types), unit secretary, transportation worker, or technician.

Hospitals are radically different from the typical church, in that they are complex in structure, made up of a variety of disciplines, and scientifically oriented with an emphasis on high technology. When the pastor leaves the church office, where she may be the

Chief Executive Officer (or at least one of the junior executives), and visits the hospital, which is the primary workplace of other professionals, it is no wonder that she may feel like an alien in a strange land. Add to that the fact that we are more likely to hear references to miracles attributed to doctors and hospitals than to pastors and churches, and it is easy to understand why some pastors might develop something of a "grasshopper complex."

Many pastors become somewhat familiar with hospitals by taking a unit of Clinical Pastoral Education in a hospital setting. A unit of CPE can help us find our way in a hospital. Some hospitals offer extended units for community clergy who have not taken CPE and cannot spend full time in a CPE program.

When pastors go to the hospital to visit parishioners, they have to determine where to park (including special parking privileges for clergy), where to get information about a parishioner's location, what visiting regulations apply (again including special privileges for clergy), and they often need to make some contact with personnel in the patient's unit before seeing that patient. Their contact person in the unit may be a head nurse (or clinical manager), charge nurse, or primary nurse. The nurse may have even more specific information on unit regulations affecting a visit with the parishioner. There are frequently gatekeepers in three areas: parking, entry into the hospital, and entry into a specific unit. No wonder pastors often feel as if they are working their way through a maze!

The purpose of this chapter is to provide some guidelines for finding the way to a parishioner with greater ease and confidence. Although there is no single roadmap for all hospitals, there are some general guidelines that may be helpful.

GETTING THE LAY OF THE LAND

The first task of the spies in Canaan was to find out what the land was like. What was its geography and climate?

I once started what I thought was to be a five-mile canoe trip at 2:00 P.M. In my quick look at the map, I interpreted numbered access points on the river as mileage indicators. After weathering a storm I arrived at my planned destination thirty-two miles downstream at 8:00 P.M. Near the end of my journey, I met two National Park rangers who had set out to find me before night fall. What is true for canoeing is true for finding one's way in the hospital as well. A good orientation to the map is time and effort well spent.

Almost every hospital has some kind of orientation for visiting clergy. Hospitals recognize the reality of clergy visitation and are concerned with both the importance of good community relations and the need to regulate visitation and protect patients. Programs of orientation provide pastors with helpful information on the policies regarding clergy visitation, as well as privileges, such as parking, special facilities, and access to information. Any pastor planning to visit patients in the hospital on a regular basis should seek such an orientation.

Frequently, persons staffing the hospital lobby information desk can tell a pastor how their particular hospital orients new clergy or can direct her to someone who does have that information. They may give you a brief orientation on the spot and invite you back for a more thorough one on a regularly scheduled date.

The orientation and regulation of visiting clergy may be the responsibility of the hospital chaplain or department of pastoral care, if the hospital has such a department. As the link between hospital and clergy, the chaplain becomes a resource for orientation to the hospital and a help in continued visitation.

Where the hospital does not have a chaplain on staff, someone is usually designated to interpret policy regarding clergy visitation. It may be the director of volunteers, an administrator, or even a representative from the local ministerial association.

BECOMING FAMILIAR WITH THE INHABITANTS
OF THE LAND

The second task of the spies Moses sent into Canaan was to size up the inhabitants. Like those spies, some pastors are over-impressed and intimidated by hospital personnel. These pastors, too, may suffer from the "grasshopper complex." Their temptation is to keep a low profile and to slip in and out of the hospital without calling attention to themselves. An understanding of the roles and functions of some key hospital personnel, however, can help the pastor to view and utilize staff as an important resource in pastoral visitation.

The hospital chaplain is a key resource. Similarities and differences make allies of parish pastor and chaplain. Pastoral work with patients becomes complementary rather than competitive. Hospital chaplains respect a pastor's privileged relationship with her parishioner and recognize that she is that person's primary pastor. They are glad to assist in her pastoral ministry.

The pastor's ministry and that of the chaplain differ. The first and perhaps the most important difference is in the relationship to a parishioner. The pastor's relationship begins prior to and continues beyond the parishioner's hospital stay. A pastor usually knows the parishioner in other situations and in roles beyond that of patient. The pastor's more complete knowledge of the person is usually an advantage, enabling more effective pastoral care to be provided over a long-term basis, with a helpful degree of continuity.

The chaplain, on the other hand, must establish a relationship, which is then confined to the hospital setting and the person's role as a patient. The advantage of the chaplain is ready access to hospital staff and resources. The chaplain is an insider and is more consistently present during the patient's stay in the hospital. The chaplain's presence is more immediate and is more likely to be available in the event of a sudden crisis. The chaplain, of course, is more familiar with the medical language and the crisis events that occur in the hospital setting.

In my own experience as pastor of a congregation, I was rarely present immediately after someone died or during an immediate crisis. I was called to plan and officiate at funerals and to provide follow-up care after a funeral or crisis event. As a chaplain I am often called to the emergency room or to one of the hospital units during a trauma or death. I am often present for the onset of grief immediately following death. However, I am rarely involved in funerals or the follow-up care of the bereaved.

These differences may complement pastoral ministry. The chaplain can keep a pastor informed regarding the diagnosis, prognosis, and current condition of a parishioner. Pastors can communicate to the chaplain under what circumstances they would like to be informed regarding events in the hospitalization of their parishioner. They may resort to the chaplain primarily as an informational resource while they provide the primary face-to-face ministry. They may also choose to make use of the chaplain as a partner in visiting and providing pastoral care in a more direct way. Occasionally, the chaplain may be the primary caregiver either in the pastor's absence or because of the nature of the pastor's relationship to a particular parishioner. Occasionally the nature of a pastor-parishioner relationship is such that pastoral care is best provided by someone else. Patients sometimes feel more secure with the relative anonymity afforded by a more temporary relationship with a hospital chaplain. They may feel they have to be on their best behavior for their pastor.

Another key person in the hospitalized patient's life is the nurse. When a pastor arrives in the unit to visit a parishioner, the pastor should identify herself and ask for the patient's nurse. Let the nurse know who you are, why you are there, and ask if there are any special procedures or precautions you should know in visiting the patient.

Nursing stations can be busy and confusing places. Staffing patterns vary. Some use a team approach in which different nurses do different tasks for a large number of patients. Others use a concept of primary nursing care in which each patient has one nurse who is responsible for the total care of the patient. In every situation one nurse in each unit will be designated the charge nurse. The charge nurse can either provide the information needed or direct you to the patient's primary nurse.

Nurses are the ultimate gatekeepers to patients. It is they who manage and provide the primary care, and spend the most time with the patient. They have the most complete picture of what is happening with the patient. They can give access to the patient and may share valuable information and perspectives on the condition and needs of the patient.

For example, pastors are often reluctant to disturb a patient who is sleeping. Perhaps the patient needs her rest. The nurse might say, "Go ahead and wake her. She needs social stimulation more than rest right now. In fact she is somewhat withdrawn and she might sleep better at night if she slept less during the day." Or the nurse might make suggestions about the best time to visit.

Occasionally an impatient or uncooperative nurse may be encountered, but most nurses appreciate the professional courtesy of your contact. They like to know who is visiting their patients.

ESTABLISHING YOURSELF

The purpose of the spies in the land of Canaan was ultimately to establish the Israelites as its inhabitants, to take over the land. Caleb countered the pessimism of the other spies and their "grasshopper complex" with the words, "Let us go up at once and occupy it, for we are well able to overcome it" (Numbers 13:30).

Pastors also need to let the hospital staff know who they are. They need to establish themselves as a part of the team whose common goal is to provide the best of care for their parishioner. Just as it is important for pastors to know the roles hospital staff play so that they can most effectively use the resources of the staff, it is also important that hospital staff learn the unique contributions pastors make to the care of the patient. That requires dialogue. As pastors participate in that kind of dialogue in the hospitals they visit regularly, health care providers will come to know pastors and to some degree what they represent. I recall one encounter I had with a cardiovascular surgeon. My immediate impression was that he did not care for religion in general and clergy in particular. Later, I discovered he was having his own struggle with faith. After the relationship was more firmly established, he said to me once, "I don't understand the spiritual, but I respect it. And I value anything that helps my patients and gives them an edge." As our dialogue continued, he increasingly consulted with me about patients and asked for my pastoral assistance, both for patients and for himself.

The pastor's prior knowledge of the patient, the patient's

prehospital experience, the patient's setting and resources may be something that all the hospital personnel (doctors, nurses, social workers, chaplains) lack. Your perspective, encompassing knowledge of what the patient was like before hospitalization and the setting to which the patient may return, may be very important to the rest of the caring team and helpful in the care of the patient.

As a parish pastor I was once involved in the hospitalization of a young parishioner who was becoming psychotic. After being called by a family member to see her one evening, I, with her permission, consulted with her physician. He and I shared our perceptions and both felt she needed to be in treatment. She informed me that she had an appointment with him the next day, and he would refer her for psychiatric treatment. He referred her to a private psychiatrist she and her husband could not afford. Later in the week they came to my study, because her condition had worsened. I discussed with them the possibility of admittance to a nearby state hospital where I had recently taken a unit of Clinical Pastoral Education and knew the staff and its treatment program rather well.

I called their physician, explained the situation, and he agreed to recommend them for hospitalization. I accompanied them to the hospital, continued to visit with them and support them through treatment, and her mental health improved immensely. Although I lacked the credentials to order a hospitalization, I had a pastoral relationship and a perspective that played an important part in influencing her appropriate treatment and sustaining her and her husband through it. The doctor knew her as a patient. I knew her as a person.

When we visit our parishioners in the hospital, we need to inform the key medical people who we are and what we are about. When situations arise that call for consultation, pastors should not be timid about seeking out the appropriate persons, be it doctor, nurse, or chaplain.

When I visited in the hospital as a pastor, I found that verbally identifying myself as the parishioner's pastor was not always enough. Especially in hospitals where I visited infrequently and was not known by the nurses. Even though I would stop at the nurses' station and introduce myself as a person's pastor making a visit, I found that another nurse might interrupt my pastoral visit. Sometimes such interruptions are unavoidable. However, in wearing just my business suit there was nothing that made me visibly or professionally recognizable. A nurse walking into the room could not distinguish me from a family member or any other visitor.

A clerical collar provides visibility and immediate visual identity, but at the time I was a pastor in a geographical area and in a denomination in which a clerical collar was not appropriate. I began using a small stole (which now may be purchased through some denominational supply houses) that I could carry in my pocket and put on as I entered a hospital room. The result was remarkable. It provided immediate visual recognition and interruptions declined.

If the pastor claims a place on the interdisciplinary team, all caregivers are enabled to work together for the benefit of the patient. Cooperation requires initiative and effective communication. The result will be a greater sense of satisfaction and a more effective pastoral ministry in the hospital setting.

Having found our way into the hospital, we examine the needs of the patients who will be the recipients of our ministry. Ministry in the emergency room, for example, calls for skills different from those required in working with patients who are comatose. The next chapter highlights patients, the unique needs they present (depending on the nature of their illness or the treatment that they are to receive), and the ways in which pastors can employ that knowledge in ministry.

CHAPTER SIX

THE PATIENT'S NEEDS

As a hospital chaplain, I am frequently present with families at times in which they receive some of the worst news that they will ever hear. Not long ago, I was paged by one of our surgeons and asked to be with him as unhappily he brought news of an inoperable metastatic cancer to the waiting family of his patient. His message was received like a death sentence, dashing all their hopes, confronting them with their worst fears. First, the numbness and disbelief, then the tears, abundant and deep. These are painful and difficult times for me. I always wish that I could be the bearer of better news. In his recent book, *Naming the Silences,* Stanley Hauerwas observes that at times such as these we confront life as it really is, not as we might wish it could be, or as we might pretend that it is. These painful times produce "silences," which are often filled with cries of pain and angry protest.[1] On these occasions, when the family pastor is present, family members often turn immediately to the pastor for advice and comfort. In the face of life's inequity and pain, we turn naturally to the Creator's representative to help us find our way through the uncertainty. Some hospital chaplains wish that pastors were more often immediately present with families at such times of crisis. When pastors are not present, we often hear from them that they are intimidated by the foreign nature of the hospital. Pastors may feel out of place in the hospital, uncertain of their role in the midst of the hospital's clinicians. While the foregoing chapter suggests systemic ways to reduce the intimidation, this chapter might help in understanding what many patients experience during their hospitalization. Some issues are common to most persons who are hospitalized, regardless of the nature of their illness. We examine these issues initially and then focus on several patient diagnoses that contain issues unique to them.

The predominant emotion experienced by patients upon entering the hospital is fear. It is present to a greater or lesser degree in all patients. Commonly, that fear takes primarily four forms.

1. The fear of separation. Admission to the hospital requires that we leave the company of those who love us and abide for a while in a land of strangers. These strangers come to us dressed in a manner different from any garb to which we are accustomed outside the hospital. They speak a language that we often do not understand. They communicate with one another in hushed tones, frequently in our presence, making us wonder what they are discussing. They tell us some of the truth, not necessarily all of it, only what seems to them to be beneficial for us. When they do not want us to hear them, they leave the room to talk about us. Is it any wonder that patients often say, "I just want to go home!" Even when the reason for hospitalization is a happy one, such as the delivery of a baby, there is still a deep desire to "be at home in my own bed."

2. The fear of dependence. The hospital is a place that teaches people—some for the first time since infancy—the meaning of dependence. We depend upon the admitting department to have a room for us, on the dietary department to feed us, on the diagnostic and therapeutic skills of the medical and nursing staff to treat us, on the training of social workers and therapists to ensure our continued healing upon discharge, on chaplains to understand our feelings and to provide pastoral support for our emotional and spiritual needs. Surgery requires us to depend on an anesthesiologist to put us to sleep and wake us up, and on a surgeon to cut us open and successfully put us back together again.

3. The fear of losing control. Upon entering the hospital, patients quickly surrender control. Loss of control begins with the "see-through" gown that is given to patients to wear. Patients eat when the hospital determines and may share a room with a stranger (who may snore loudly or watch television all night). Everyone from the newspaper sales person to the attending physician enters the room without so much as a knock. Body secretions are examined and measured. Control of the most vital functions, including stopping and starting the heart, is surrendered to others. Children are particularly vulnerable to the fear of losing control. To the degree that they can be included in the decisions that are made about them, they tend to do better emotionally.

4. The fear of pain and death. Many persons worry about their ability to tolerate pain. Males who have been schooled to ignore pain may fear being judged weak or whiny. Beyond the pain is the ever-present fear of death. Patients often remark that "hospitals are places where people go to die." Even ostensibly happy occasions, such as childbirth, are marked by the concern that "the baby will have all of his fingers and toes."

All these fears add up to taking a person out of a home in which she feels secure and placing her into a stressful and strange environment in which she feels threatened, the victim of forces beyond her control. Given the known deleterious effects that such stress can have upon persons, there are some who feel that the fact that people regain their health in the hospital is less a testimony to the skill of the medical profession and more the evidence of the remarkable resilience of the human body and spirit. Truly we have been "wonderfully made" (Psalm 139:14).

In addition to the fears just named, there are particular diagnoses or units in the hospital that engender fears and effects unique to them. An understanding of these effects can facilitate ministry.

THE EMERGENCY ROOM

The emergency room (ER) can be one of the most frightening and frustrating places in the hospital. It is frightening because its name is synonymous with extreme crisis, perceived threat of loss of life. All the fears just mentioned are magnified in the ER. It is frustrating in that family members are cut off from their loved ones, who are often being treated by someone other than the familiar and reassuring family physician whose longstanding relationship to the family engenders a high degree of confidence. The characteristic "triage" system by which ER staff determine priority of treatment may leave a patient and his family waiting while others who arrive later are treated first. In a setting that can be chaotic, the pastor may be the one person who can bring a calm and comforting presence.

Ministry in the ER requires awareness of and training in the skills of crisis intervention. Although only an introduction can be included here, there are many good texts that can help train a pastor in the skills of working with people at times of intense crisis.[2]

A crisis is the result of an event seen to be so threatening that it renders a person unable to cope by usual methods and feeling at the mercy of events beyond his control. Included in that definition are primarily two elements: the threatening event and the inability to cope.

There is little or nothing that the pastor can do to change the threatening event. She can help people to talk about the event, to share their feelings about it, and to become aware of the effect that the event is having on them. Ministry at this point may be made up primarily of listening and helping the patient or patient's family members to talk about their fearful feelings. A sensitive pastor may be the linking person who is able to facilitate the flow of information between treatment and waiting rooms.

There is much that the pastor can do to assist people who are struggling to cope with an emergency. Crises are sudden; they happen without warning. There is a randomness to them that makes them appear unfair or discriminatory. Crises foster feelings of confusion, helplessness, dependency, and extreme vulnerability. In the face of such events, persons may react in various ways. They may withdraw or become actively verbal; they may quietly pace the floor or openly express anger at everyone, particularly at those who are trying to help them. They may raise questions regarding the treatment or blame others for the crisis. In rare cases, persons may become hostile and act out their feelings in a violent or threatening manner.

Pastors can help those involved to cope by remembering that, in the midst of a crisis, there is a need for structure. Pastors can assist in creating structure and order in a number of ways.

1. They should become actively involved with the family and circumstances immediately by helping persons to talk about the situation and vent their feelings.

2. They should remain warm and calm, communicating a sense of control, helping persons to feel that the pastor can be depended on for help and understanding.

3. They should attempt to control the environment to the degree that this is possible for them. If a family is actively grieving, a crowded waiting room is not the most appropriate place for expressing such feelings. Most hospitals have a small family room to which families can be brought for privacy. Almost all ER's have a coffee pot somewhere. There may be support persons who can be summoned by phone to be with the family in their grief.

4. To paraphrase a common realtor's motto: "The three most important aspects of crisis intervention are listening, listening, and listening." Persons in crisis have a deep need to know that they are being heard. The pastor may often be the first person who is able to actively listen to the feelings of a patient or her family members. In an emergency, the medical staff may simply be too busy to listen effectively.

5. The family can be helped to cope. Persons in crisis commonly ask, What should I do? They are unusually open to attempts at helping them find means of coping. It may be possible to help them explore past crisis experiences and recall what helped them cope during those times. They can be helped to search for new or alternative methods. Ineffective means of coping may gently be exposed as such. In the event of death, persons may well depend on the pastor's expertise in determining what they will need to do to begin preparing for the funeral.

6. Be open to the opportunity to use spiritual resources. Gathering a fearful family together for prayer may help to calm them. In the face of death, the pastor can help them view the body

of their loved one, vent their feelings of despair, and focus on good memories that remain. A prayer of committal, if appropriate, may help them give over to God the care of their loved one.

Perhaps it is appropriate at this point to note that pastors can help families prepare for emergencies well in advance. In addition to preparing advance directives—living wills and durable powers of attorney for health care—families can file with the church office forms that contain information needed at the time of death. One such form is contained in appendix A.

INTENSIVE CARE

The intensive care unit (ICU) may well be the most frightening place in the entire hospital. This is best understood when one attempts, as much as possible, to put himself in the place of the patient.

Difficulties are encountered immediately at the point of communication. Patients are often intubated and attached to a ventilator, which breathes for them. As the breathing tube runs through the larynx, the ability to speak is taken away from the patient. In many hospitals, ventilated patients may be placed in loose restraint, preventing them from removing their breathing tube, preventing them also from using their hands and arms to assist in communication. Compression boots, which assist in preventing the throwing off of blood clots, may be attached to the legs. In other words, the patient remains largely immobile, unable to communicate, aware of his surroundings, but unaware of the meaning of what he hears around him. Intravenous pumps, ventilators, Swan-Ganz catheters, and other kinds of ICU equipment are monitored; changes in their function trigger alarms the patient can hear and which may cause him to wonder if there is something going wrong with his condition. All around him are other ICU patients. Cardiac arrests are common in an ICU. Few things are more frightening to a patient than hearing a cardiopulmonary resuscitation (CPR) attempt going on nearby. The hurried movements of the code team, the conversation in which they engage, the sounds of suction and defibrillators, the beeping of heart monitors or lack of it, and the awareness that death has claimed the life of a fellow patient—these and other critical events take place and are witnessed by a patient, who can only lie flat on his back, unable to communicate his anxiety, unable even to ask for the reassurance he needs to feel more secure.

In the ICU, dependence is total. Patients are fed by tube. Waste products are removed by tube. Every bodily function is scrutinized by ICU personnel. Patients are examined constantly; vital signs are taken often. Sleep deprivation is common in a situation in which there is constant activity and light, around the clock. Except for family members who come to visit (only in carefully monitored numbers and for short periods of time), there is little or no outside stimulation. Technicians wander in and out of the room to check equipment and may not even communicate with the patient. The patient feels she is in a fish bowl with absolutely no privacy. Along with all of this is the ever-present fear of death.

A common complication, very distressing to patients and family members, is ICU psychosis, a state of disorientation and confusion that may begin "to appear in patients who spend more than 5 to 7 days in an ICU."[3] Characterized by orientation problems, memory difficulties, and confusion as to time and place, the patient cannot understand why nursing staff constantly ask him such questions as, Do you know where you are? Family members fear that something has happened to make their loved one's condition worse. Once a patient is moved out of intensive care and begins to get more sleep, the condition frequently disappears.

Patients commonly respond to these conditions in a number of ways. Some become extremely compliant, willing to do anything that is asked of them by the staff, afraid to alienate anyone on whom they depend for survival. Other patients respond by attempting to regain control. They may be "on their light" constantly, asking nursing staff for help with the simplest of tasks. Still other patients become angry and manipulative, commonly finding fault with everything and everyone around them.

Ministry to ICU patients is best kept short and simple. The communication problem with intubated patients can be countered to some degree by remembering to ask only yes and no kinds of questions, to which the patient can nod a response. Patients who are kept ventilated for long periods of time can be assisted by being given a clipboard and pencil, or encouraged to trace words letter-by-letter in the palm of the pastor's hand.

Reassurance is a necessary component of recovery. Patients need to be told how good they look and how well they are doing, but not in an insincere or shallow manner. Patients may be quick to respond to such a comment with, "How can you say that? I look awful." I may well respond to that by noting accurately, "Well, you look like someone who has just had major surgery; that's the way you're supposed to look. But your color is good; your eyes are bright; you're alert. You're really coming along well." Such a reassurance, which does not beg what is obvious to the patient, is often experienced by that patient as supportive.

One of the most important components of ministry is touch. People are often daunted by the tubes and wires that are attached to ICU patients. Hands and wrists may have several intravenous lines running into a number of heparin-locks. Family members are sometimes reluctant to touch a patient's hand for fear of hurting her. Such reluctance robs a patient of vital support. In addition, patients who have diseases such as cancer or AIDS quickly become aware of other people's fear of contracting the disease by touching them. Irrational though such fears may be, they exist, and the avoidance of touch contributes to a patient's sense of isolation. Not long ago, one of the patients to whom I was ministering was not doing well after heart surgery. He was restless, thrashing around in his bed, and giving his nurse great concern about his lack of rest. I sat with the man and held his hand for almost an hour as he slowly settled down into a fitful sleep. Words did not need to be spoken. A couple of weeks later, when he was well on the road to recovery, he asked one morning, "Did I imagine it, or did you sit with me and hold my hand for a while one day when I was in intensive care?" His gratitude was deep.

Finally, visits to the ICU should be kept short. Most pastors are aware of this, but occasionally a pastor will come to visit whose stay outlasts his welcome. Five minutes is generally a good guide.

SURGERY

All the fears mentioned early in this chapter are common to patients scheduled to undergo surgery. The most common fear that I encounter as I call on patients pre-operatively is associated with the anesthesiologist. Patients are very open with their fear that, once they are put to sleep, they may not awaken again. Anesthesia is an experience in being out of control, of having to trust your life to someone other than yourself. The fear may be greater or smaller depending on the degree to which the patient is or is not a highly controlled or controlling individual. Sometimes it is helpful to assist a patient in exploring her control needs as a means of understanding the fear of anesthesia.

Five types of surgical procedures carry fears that are unique to them. (1) Exploratory surgery, such as a biopsy or laparotomy, carries the fear that "they're going to find something." Often, it is the discovery of cancer that is feared. (2) Cancer procedures carry the fear that a known cancer may be found to be so widespread as to be inoperative, or located in a position in which it is impossible to remove all of the tumor. Commonly designated "open and close" cases, such surgery brings with it the fear of painful suffering and death. (3) Some surgeries threaten the patient with a change in life-style. Coronary artery bypass surgery, for example, raises the question of whether a patient will be able to continue to live as he has in the past. Much postsurgical depression in heart patients has to do with this issue. Patients fear that the slightest exertion may cause their readmission to the hospital. Sensitive counseling can often help them discover that, though some changes may need to be made, they will probably be able to do even more than they have in the past. (4) Various gynecological surgeries raise questions related to sexuality, appearance, and identity. Women undergoing radical mastectomy, for example, wonder about their appearance in clothing or the possible loss of attractiveness to a sexual partner. Males undergoing prostate surgery bring concern for impaired sexual functioning. (5) Transplant procedures carry the very real fear that the body will reject the transplanted organ. The rejection of a bone marrow transplant may well mean death for a patient with leukemia.

Patients' comments indicate their response to these fears. They may play down the surgery: "I'm just going in overnight for a *little* procedure" (not "surgery"). More often seen is denial: "This doesn't bother me at all; I can't wait to get it done." They become highly talkative or jocular as a means of distancing themselves from the surgery and its fear. An apparently resigned fatalism may be present: "It's got to be done; there's nothing I can do about it." Such patients have more anger and resistance than resignation and may be helped by an examination of these feelings and a focus upon what benefits may come to them through the surgery. Occasionally, patients may become deeply depressed in advance of surgery. This is particularly troubling to family members whose need is for their loved one to go into surgery as "up" as possible.

The focus on shortened hospital stay has resulted in many surgical patients being admitted to the hospital on the day of their surgery. Many surgical procedures are performed on an outpatient basis, with patients no longer admitted to the hospital at all. Although this has made it harder for pastors and chaplaincy staff to conduct pre-operative ministry, visiting patients prior to their surgery continues to be of vital importance.

Several guides provide the focus for presurgical ministry. (1) Ministry should be responsive, not directive. Not all patients need, or even want, to see a pastor prior to surgery. A sensitive pastor recognizes the patient who may feel threatened by a pastoral visit and is not offended by being dismissed. In compelling a reluctant parishioner to accept a visit, the pastor only confirms his need to be needed. (2) Pastors should be alert for the nuances in the emotional needs of the patient. If a patient is coping through the mechanism of denial, it is important to allow her to do so. We have no license to pull the rug of denial out from under a patient. To the degree that it is possible to help patients ventilate feelings, the pastor can provide a valuable service. Too often, family members deliver shallow reassurance at the point of a patient-expressed fear. Instead of the empty pastoral phrase, "I'm sure everything is going to be fine," the patient might better benefit from the sensitivity of the pastor who can agree with him: "It is scary to face this surgery, isn't it.'' (3) A pastor should attempt to enter into a patient's fear and to stand with her there, sharing the patient's feelings, hurting with her, exploring the hope for a better future, entering into the meaning of death. Henri Nouwen reminds us that ''anyone who willingly enters into the pain of a stranger is truly a remarkable person.''[4] (4) A pastor should be alert for issues of external-internal locus of control. Patients feel much more like victims to the degree that they perceive events coming to them externally, beyond their control. To the degree that they can be helped to see themselves playing a part in what happens to them, experiencing a degree of internal control over events, they tend to feel better about their circumstances. Children, in particular, are thought to take a more active part in coping with their situation to the degree that they feel that they have some voice in the matter.[5] Without taking away a patient's valid feelings, it can be helpful to (5) help patients focus on compensatory gains and past coping strategies. What good will come to them as a result of the surgery? How have they coped in the past when they've felt threatened? (6) Pastors should be aware of the power of spiritual resources and use them when appropriate. Persons facing surgery may have a need for confession, to ease the burden of guilt from their conscience in the event that they do not survive the surgery. The sacrament of Holy Communion brings the forgiveness and acceptance of God. The fact that patients are NPO (''non per ora'') and restricted from eating or drinking in advance of surgery is usually not an impediment to the sacrament. A small piece of wafer tinctured in grape juice can suffice. If there is any doubt about this, a question to the physician or nurse can resolve the doubt. Finally, properly employed, prayer is a resource that carries calming and cathartic power. A patient's *admitted* fears can be lifted up and offered to God along with a request for God's presence during the surgery, bringing about the miracles of healing through the skills God gives the medical staff, the courage and faith of the patient, and the love and support of family and friends. To the degree that pastors are sensitive to patient needs, a valuable ministry of support can be provided in the face of frightening uncertainty.

STROKE AND COMA

There is probably no patient who seems to present so many challenges to ministry as the patient who is unresponsive. We are highly verbal individuals, and most ministry follows that form, offering the right words at the right time in mutual give-and-take with the patient. When that option is removed, we may stand mute and puzzled, perhaps even unwilling to visit a comatose patient, either out of our own discomfort at being in a position in which we cannot *do* something tangible, or out of the belief that the patient cannot benefit from a visit.

Coma is frequently the immediate result of having suffered a stroke (more properly, CVA or cardiovascular accident). The presence of coma does not necessarily imply a bad prognosis.[6] As the effects of the stroke recede, it is not unusual to see patients recover from a comatose state. There may or may not be a degree of residual impairment.

The effects of a stroke can be very problematic for the patient as well as for her family. There may be personality changes; persons who were pleasant and easy-going may become hostile and recalcitrant. They may lose control of bodily functions. Damage to the emotional control center of the brain is common, resulting in patients who laugh and cry at inappropriate moments. One of the very frustrating effects is that one in which patients retain the ability to speak, but lose the ability to form meaningful words. They know what they want to say, but only nonsense syllables emerge from their mouth when they attempt to speak. To the degree that persons are rendered unable to do many of the things that they have always done, there may be real grieving for the life that they have lost. Dependency, loss of self-esteem, and a heightened sense of uselessness may be present as well. Patients may respond to these symptoms by either trying desperately, and sometimes inappropriately, to be involved in family conversations or events, or withdrawing into a lonely and irritable silence. Some may revert to childlike behavior, forcing the family to consider the need for skilled nursing home placement.

When coma is present, it is important to remember that a patient retains the ability to hear even if he is unable to respond.[7] This offers opportunities for care to the pastor and the patient's family. I make a practice of holding the hands of comatose patients and praying quietly with them. Poetry and scripture can be read. A pastor friend of mine brought a small tape player and ear-phones to his wife who was comatose for a long period of time. Each day, as he journeyed with her through her illness, he played to her tapes of music that she loved.

Patients who recover from coma and stroke may enter a rehabilitation unit for training in independence. Ministry at this point requires great patience at the fumbling attempts that patients may make in their effort to speak or to do things previously easy for them. It is important to facilitate the venting of their feelings while at the same time encouraging them to do as much for themselves as possible. Though they may behave as such, it is important to refrain from treating them like children.

AIDS AND CANCER

At the time of this writing, we have just passed the tenth anniversary of the June 1981 announcement of the discovery of AIDS by the Atlanta-based federal Center for Disease Control. Since that time, more than 175,000 Americans have contracted AIDS and 109,000 have died of the disease. AIDS is now the "leading killer of women ages 15 to 44 in New York and New Jersey, in addition to being the No. 1 cause of death in men ages 25 to 44 in New York, Los Angeles, and San Francisco."[8] It is an epidemic of frightening proportions.

Though suffering from different diseases, AIDS and cancer patients share many dynamics in common, making it possible to treat them together. Both diagnoses tend to be heard as a death sentence. Both involve protracted treatment programs that subject patient and family members to an emotional roller-coaster ride. Both diseases have a distancing quality to them that makes family members and former friends suddenly hold themselves at arm's length, increasing the patient's sense of isolation. Both diseases may have physically disfiguring effects on their victims, frequently causing patients to waste away before the eyes of those who care for them. In addition, though it is contracted in ways other than through homosexual activity or IV-drug use, AIDS still carries a moral stigma in the minds of many people.

The emotional dynamics experienced by AIDS and cancer patients tend to be similar to those experienced by anyone facing a life-threatening illness. Initially explored in Elisabeth Kübler-Ross's well-known *On Death and Dying*,[9] these emotional dynamics have become familiar to caregivers who work with terminally ill patients.[10] These dynamics may be divided into a number of stages:

1. Shock, made up of disbelief at the diagnosis. A feeling of numbness.

2. Relief. More common to AIDS patients who suspected that they were HIV-positive, but were living in the anxiety of not knowing.

3. Anger. Brought about by the discovery that there is no cure or that the treatment program will require them to substantially change their life-style. Anger may be directed at persons who react negatively toward them, or at God for failing to protect them.

4. Guilt, out of believing that the disease might have been avoided by living differently. A cancer patient said recently, "Well, I refused to quit smoking; I guess I got what I deserved." Both AIDS and cancer patients may feel guilt at becoming a burden to family and friends.

5. Decreased self-esteem. Avoidance reactions of others may cause patients to feel unclean. In AIDS patients, prejudicial reactions of others tend to reinforce this.

6. Loss of identity. The result of feeling different in appearance, personality, or life-style. Both AIDS and cancer patients may feel socially and sexually unacceptable. In AIDS patients, a lover may leave out of a fear of contamination.

7. Loss of security. The world is no longer experienced as a safe place in which to live. For cancer patients in remission, every ache and pain raises the suspicion that the disease has returned.

8. Loss of personal control. A patient's entire life may now seem to be directed by his disease. Personal plans may have to be

made to fit between trips to the hospital for treatment, or canceled because of the severe side-effects of drugs.

9. Fear. A constant companion. There may be fear of the treatment, of the recurrence of the disease, of the inability to cope with what the future may bring.

10. Sadness and depression, brought about by the knowledge that events are beyond the control of the patient, that suffering and death may be imminent regardless of treatment.

11. Obsession and compulsion. The patient may find all her waking moments are spent thinking about the illness or about dying. The body may be checked constantly for signs of renewed illness.

12. Positive adjustment. The point at which *some* patients come to terms with their illness, accept its inevitability, and determine to live on a one-day-at-a-time basis. They may join self-help or support groups to help them cope, or they may withdraw and bitterly resign themselves to that which they cannot change.

The above "stages" are not mileposts past which all patients move. Some patients may never progress past the initial anger. Others may come to a point of dying with a profound sense of having lived as meaningfully as possible; they may die with an expectant sense of God's reaching out to them with a new life, free of pain and sadness.

Pastoral care to persons with AIDS or cancer may be crucial to helping them cope. Above all, the pastor should be present to the patient, providing the opportunity for the patient to vent his feelings and be heard. We need to remember to physically touch such patients. Jesus frequently put his hands upon those who came to him for healing. The social stigma isolating AIDS patients can be overcome only by the demonstrated physical caring by those who know that we are all brothers and sisters in God's love. We need to be prepared to commit ourselves to a long period of ministry to cancer and AIDS patients. The disease may go into remission, only to return with a vengeance. The roller-coaster ride of emotions may extend over a period of years. Pastors should help patients find support among persons whose common experience can bridge the gap of isolation felt by terminally ill patients. We need to be alert to suicidal ideation, helping patients find meaning and purpose in coping, urging them to make the greatest possible use of the life that they have. Pastors can help patients prepare advance directives and determine how they are going to die. Treatment decisions can be made in advance. Family and friends can be counseled and helped to communicate with and support their loved one. They can be helped to focus on their dreams and work out ways in which some of their hopes can be realized during the time that they have remaining. Pastors can preach and teach in the effort to counter the prejudicial societal attitudes that isolate and alienate AIDS patients.

Throughout all of their ministry to AIDS and cancer patients, pastors must come to terms with their need to see patients benefit from their ministry. There is a frustration in working with severely depressed or terminally ill patients that can cause pastors to avoid being with the very patients who need them the most. One clergyperson said it well:

Oh, how we want our patients to feel better after we have visited them! I learned that this is *my* need, and not necessarily that of the patient. "Has my visit been a big help to you?"—that is the tacit question we clergy ask. Better to ask: "Have I heard you? Have I given you the opportunity to say what you want to say, and not what I want you to say? Have I been able to confront you in illness without undermining your dignity? Have I allowed you to reach out? Have I conveyed the knowledge that you are safe with me—safe in whatever you want to say, whatever you want to do, whatever you want to be?" Finally, I must convey hope—not a pollyanna hope, but a genuine faith in the future.[11]

Such an attitude can help us minister in the presence of a disease whose course we cannot change and enable us to help persons approach their illness with dignity and their death with hope. We look now at the resources that the pastor brings to this effort.

CHAPTER SEVEN

THE PASTOR'S SPIRITUAL RESOURCES

I saw Joanne for the first time when she arrived on a gurney in the surgical holding area. Set up across the hall from the operating room, the area allows family members to be with patients right up to the time they enter the operating room. Joanne was alone. I'm uncomfortable when I see patients come alone for surgery. Surgery is a frightening experience. The supportive presence of family or friends can ease some of the fear. I introduced myself to her and soon learned that she was frightened. Because of the need to care for their young children, her husband had been unable to come to the hospital to be with Joanne. She was able to cry with me, allowing some of the tension to escape. As I held her hand, she told me of her fear of being anesthetized and of her concern that the surgeon would find that the tumor in her breast had spread to her lymph nodes. Because she was alone, I spent a few more minutes with her, holding her hand and listening. Finally, when it was time to go, she asked for prayer. As she left she said, "Thanks for being here; I feel better."

Such contacts with patients are common enough. This one had a postscript that made it unique. About three weeks later, I received from the hospital's administrator a copy of a letter that Joanne had written to him, expressing her appreciation for the hospital personnel who had made her time of treatment more tolerable. She specifically mentioned how the chaplain who had taken the time to be with her prior to the surgery had helped to ease the fear that she was feeling.

Joanne's case provides illustration of the power contained in the spiritual resources that are available to pastor and patient. Paul Pruyser has written cogently of the need for pastors to bring to patients the spiritual resources that their training provides and for which parishioners turn to them for help.[1] There was a time when pastors contended valiantly for recognition of the role played by the spirit in healing. That is no longer the case. Modern holistic health care recognizes that healing is a team effort, made up not only of the talents and resources of clinicians but containing also the spiritual resources brought to illness by a patient. Much has been written in support of those who work with a patient's spirit.[2]

George Paterson has written of his conviction that illness is a spiritual crisis in which "the word [spiritual] does not mean some inner part of the person which is relatively independent of the body or the mind. Rather it is used here to point to the wholeness and potential unity of the human being—body and mind, feelings and behavior, meanings and relationships."[3] Paterson notes how a patient's spiritual integrity is threatened by attacks of fear, anxiety, emptiness, depression, loneliness, isolation, shame, guilt, and anger. The pastor uniquely brings the spiritual resources to counter the influence of these experiences. Fear and anxiety can be met with the confidence engendered by faith; emptiness and depression can be eased as a patient's life is given meaning; loneliness and isolation may disappear as a patient feels herself part of a larger supportive community of faith; guilt, shame, and anger can be met by the forgiveness extended by God to all of us through the life, death, and resurrection of Jesus Christ. The spiritual resources available to pastor and patient take five very concrete forms: touch, confession, prayer, scripture, and the sacramental acts.

TOUCH

We need look no farther than the example of Jesus himself to see touch employed in the act of healing. Matthew's story of the leper is typical. When the leper came to Jesus with a plea for healing,

Jesus "stretched out his hand and touched him" (8:3). He touched Peter's mother-in-law (8:15), the eyes of those who were blind (20:34), and others. He took the hand of the sleeping child (Luke 8:54). One of the most humble and meaningful lessons taught his disciples came when he washed their feet (John 13). Other people touched him (Luke 8:46) and were healed. Belief in his Resurrection came through his invitation to his disciples to touch him (Luke 24:39).

Similarly, the apostles employed touch in healing (Acts 3:7, 5:12, 28:8). The church adopted the laying-on-of-hands as a means of sharing the Holy Spirit (Acts 8:18-19), as an act of ordination (6:6, 13:3), and as a means of conveying a spiritual gift (I Timothy 4:14). The value of touching has been retained today in churches through acts such as the benedictory passing of the peace, the laying-on-of-hands, the sacrament of baptism.

In a clinical setting such as the hospital, touch can be a powerful help in healing. Physical contact with another person reminds the patient that he is not alone. Touch brings with it a sense of connectedness in which a patient is put in touch with the community of faith represented by the pastor and is aware of the depth of support that underlies the patient's attempt at healing. Touch conveys acceptance, warmth, and intimacy. In patients with diseases such as AIDS or cancer, touch may serve to reassure them that they are not rejected, despite the nature of their illness, out of an irrational fear of contamination.

CONFESSION

The word *confession* conveys a vision of a penitent entering a closet to speak in hushed tones to a priest about her need for repentance. Confession should come out of the closet, for it is a most significant spiritual resource. Not long ago, I responded to a nurse's page to visit a patient who had expressed to her a desire to see a priest before going for major surgery. There was no priest available to us on such short notice. I expressed to the patient my willingness to hear his confession if he felt comfortable in sharing it with a United Methodist pastor. His need had less to do with orientation to a particular denomination and more to do with ridding himself of a burden in advance of surgery. It was not the first time I had heard a confession, then expressed to a patient God's promise of forgiveness, and communicated God's acceptance through my own presence with the patient.

Jesus stressed the value of the individual confession of sins. It can be found in the story of the prodigal son (Luke 15:18) as well as the parable of the Pharisee and the tax collector (Luke 18:10). The plea for forgiveness is a central part of the prayer that Jesus taught us to pray (Matthew 6:12). In today's world, confession forms an integral part of Alcoholics Anonymous' 12-step program toward recovery.

Time and again, Catholic and Protestant patients have expressed to me and to their pastors a sense of regret over deeds done, relationships shattered, or promises broken. Usually, this happens in advance of a life-threatening event, such as major surgery. Those of a cynical bent may say, ''Yes, there are no atheists in foxholes.'' As in virtually any ritual, there is danger that confession might be ''interpreted by more naive congregants as an act of magic, with automatic saving power, as if God could be manipulated by it.''[4] Genuine faith, however, goes beyond this kind of pathology and emerges with a deep confidence in being able to handle whatever may come. ''Even though I walk through the valley of the shadow of death, I fear no evil; for thou art with me'' (Psalm 23:4).

To the pastor, as to no one else, is given the opportunity to bring healing through confession. In those moments when the weary pastor wonders how effective his ministry is in the face of the tangible benefits brought by other members of the healing team, he would do well to ask himself when the last time was he heard a parishioner offer to confess to her doctor.

PRAYER

Prayer is one of the most powerful of religious resources, requiring great care in its use. We may pray with a person only to discover later that the prayer was interpreted by that person to mean that she was more ill than she really knew! Prayer can be very cathartic for a frightened patient. It is common to see prayer move persons to tears and free them to share anxious feelings.

It is possible to abuse prayer. Struggling with our own agendas, wishing that a talkative patient would recognize that we have other persons to visit, we may aggressively suggest, ''Well, why don't we share a prayer together, and then I'll see you tomorrow.'' In so doing, not only have we rejected a patient's need to be heard, but we have also violated one of the purposes of prayer, the summing-up of feelings and the offering of those feelings to God.

It is also possible to abuse prayer by making it a means of saying what the patient has refused to say. Once again, our agenda gets in the way. We hear a patient say that there is always hope, even though we see little basis for the belief, and we wish the patient would come to grips with the fact—so plain to us—that she is going to die. We have a need to help a patient prepare for death and, out of *our* need, not the patient's, we speak in *our* prayer of imminent death. We go away from the patient, feeling that we have achieved something, when possibly all that we have accomplished is the creating of uneasiness or fear.

Another problem that we may experience in the use of prayer is that of seeing it as a means of avoiding a subject that we would rather not confront in our conversation with the patient. Again, it is our own feelings, or agenda, that intrude. If a pastor has not come to terms with her own mortality, she may very well respond to a dying parishioner's fear of death with a comment such as, ''Oh, you're not going to die,'' thereby denying what everyone else—including the patient—believes to be true. That discomfort may even move us to bring a conversation to a close with the suggestion of prayer, thereby denying the parishioner the opportunity to talk through his own fear of dying.

In the course of my ministry, I have found it of value to visit with patients on the afternoon or evening before they are to have surgery. If the surgery is particularly critical in nature, prayer at such a time can serve to buoy the patient and her family. I have learned to say that I *routinely* like to share prayer with persons before surgery, and I *ask* the patient's permission to do this. Most of the time, patients are eager for prayer on their behalf. On rare occasions, however, when a person indicates that she would rather I not pray, it is important to respect that decision. For all we know, the hospital chaplain may already have visited and prayed with the patient.

The content of prayer also is important. I try to include the fears that have surfaced during my conversation with the patient, the questions that have been raised, the uncertainty that is evident. On occasion, when I sense a genuine fear just below the surface of the patient's words, I will lift that up as well. But great care must be taken to avoid saying that which the patient does not want said. Such a prayer, sensitively offered, can help to release patients from their fear.

In circumstances where death is imminent, it is appropriate to pray for God's support in time of pain, for help in trusting God's care, for belief that God shares our suffering with us, and to express our thanks that God is with the person that we love, helping that person to know that he is not alone. When death is very near, I have found the ancient benediction from Numbers 6:24-26 to be meaningful:

> The Lord bless you and keep you:
> The Lord make his face to shine
> upon you, and be gracious to
> you:
> The Lord lift up his countenance
> upon you, and give you peace.

One of the most meaningful points in our ministry at which prayer can help to heal is following the death of a patient. Prayer can express our thanks to God for the life and love of the person who has died, thereby summing up the feelings that family members want to share but may feel reluctant to voice in the awkwardness of the moment. A prayer may commend the care of the deceased to God and ask for support for those who remain. Where the death has left us with anger and unanswered questions, we may freely offer that anger and direct those questions to God, even to sharing feelings of bitterness that may be directed at God.

At the time of death, it is important to remember those hospital staff who have cared for the deceased. I invite them to be present and include a prayer of thanks for the care that they offered to the deceased. Often, staff persons have played an important role in the life of the one who has died, and their presence or feelings should not be left out at the end of the struggle.

The pastor is always present as a sensitive shepherd. Prayer can be one of the most significant resources enabling that presence. Should the pastor feel uncertain about the content of prayer with the sick or deceased, in addition to denominational books of worship there are ample resources available to provide help.[5] One such resource is "Ritual with the Dying," in *Ritual in a New Day*.[6]

SCRIPTURE

Charles L. Rice reminds us that "the earliest accounts of the church's life show us people meeting to eat and drink, to pray and sing, and in this context to read Scripture and hear from the presbyter."[7] When we bring the Bible into the hospital, we avail ourselves and our patients of a powerful spiritual resource. Not long ago, I called on a woman who asked me if there was a Bible available in her hospital room. I found the Bible in one of the drawers of her bedstand and offered it to her. She said, "No, I'd like you to read it to me." I asked her whether there were some favorite passages that she would like to hear. After reading two of her choice, I read parts of Paul's great hymn of assurance in Romans 8. As Paul reminded us that nothing in all of creation would be able to come between us and the love of Christ, she said to me, "That's what I needed to know." I asked, "What did you need to know?" She replied, "That no matter what happens to me, God will be there."

God is eminently able to bring about healing independent of our agenda or intents. One of the ways in which that takes place is through the reading of Scripture. Scripture itself has the power to mediate God's presence. The reading of Scripture links us to generations of Christians who have gone before us, reminding us that we are part of a strong tradition of faithful support. Similarly,

Scripture helps us take the long view of things, knowing that God has been present in the suffering and death of persons long before us, and will continue to be long after us. That assurance in itself is sufficient to quiet a restless and uncertain patient who is near death. There is a familiarity to certain passages of Scripture that enables them to comfort as nothing else is able to do. Those who need courage in the face of uncertainty may be reminded that

> God is our refuge and strength,
>   a very present help in trouble.
> Therefore we will not fear though the earth
>   should change,
>   though the mountains shake in the heart
>   of the sea. (Psalm 46:1-2)

In the face of death, there are few passages that link us as solidly to Christ's promise of continuing care as his advice to his disciples in advance of his own death:

Let not your hearts be troubled; believe in God, believe also in me. In my Father's house are many rooms; if it were not so, would I have told you that I go to prepare a place for you? And when I go and prepare a place for you, I will come again and will take you to myself, that where I am you may be also. (John 14:1-3)

In cases in which a patient has experienced long and deep suffering, one of the passages that have brought great comfort both to the dying patient and to her family is the reminder that

the dwelling of God is with [humans]. He will dwell with them, and they shall be his people, and God himself will be with them; he will wipe away every tear from their eyes, and death shall be no more, neither shall there be mourning nor crying nor pain any more, for the former things have passed away. (Revelation 21:3-4)

Although we may share Scripture personally with patients, often it is more effective to make the Scripture available to them to read as they are able. Devotional booklets such as *The Upper*

Room[8] have the advantage of being small, fitting easily into or on the patient's bed tray table. The American Bible Society publishes attractive scripture leaflets. Those that celebrate particular seasons of the church year, such as Easter and Christmas, serve to help a hospitalized parishioner feel in touch with the church, even if he is unable to be physically present.

THE SACRAMENTS

The sacraments of Eucharist and Baptism represent two of the most meaningful spiritual resources available to pastor and patient. Kenneth Mitchell reminds us that "for many Christians, the sacraments are the primary meeting place of ritual and pastoral care. Many sacraments are symbolic reenactments of some event in the life and ministry of Jesus. Although words accompany, and to some extent give specific meanings to, sacramental acts, sacraments convey meanings 'too deep for words.' ''[9] It is out of such a need for meaning that patients commonly request the sacrament of the Eucharist prior to undergoing a serious medical procedure. I can verbally reassure a patient that she is forgiven by God and accepted as a child of God, but it is the Eucharist that provides the knowledge at a deep, experiential level that the body of Christ has been given for her. I can speak of the special kind of love that Jesus had for little children, but it is the sacrament of Baptism that enables parents to feel that a dying child will be cared for by God. The sacraments are the enacted word of God.

The Eucharist contains several meanings helpful to pastors who are calling on hospitalized parishioners. It may be seen as a direct link to the support of the congregation represented by the pastor. The elements may be associated with food and drink, with spiritual nurture. With Roman Catholics, the sacrament is often linked to confession and to the restoring of a right relationship with God. In Protestantism that link does not exist in the same form, but the sacrament still tends to be seen by many as the act in which God's forgiveness is given and acceptance extended. As such, the sacrament is often requested prior to major surgery. It becomes the form by which persons are able to confess their guilt, be assured of forgiveness, and go into surgery feeling that, come what may, all will be well between them and God. It is obvious that care must be taken in the administering of the sacrament when such meanings are associated with it. The pastor who routinely comes calling with the elements will, sooner or later, encounter a frightened parishioner who assumes that the pastor would not be bringing the elements unless that parishioner were dying. Careful preparation and conversation beforehand can be undertaken to ensure proper understanding and elimination of the magical aspect in which God may be seen to be manipulated by the sacrament.

When bringing the sacrament to hospitalized patients, it is important to keep the ritual short. I prefer to follow an outline such as this:

> Greeting
> Scripture Reading
> Conversation About the Meaning of the Sacrament
> Prayer of Consecration
> Sharing the Elements with Words of Institution
> Prayer of Thanksgiving

Where patients are under an NPO (nothing by mouth) restriction, the sacrament can almost always be given by sharing just a little piece of tinctured wafer. If there is any doubt, check with the patient's nurse.

The sacrament of Baptism is often seen primarily as the act which ensures entry into God's family of faith. I encounter many people of all faiths who feel that baptism is essential for salvation. This becomes particularly troublesome at the point at which baptism is sought for someone who has died. In my own tradition, baptism is seen as an act in which persons are initiated into the fellowship of Christ, and the gathered congregation agrees to play a role in nurturing that person, something obviously impossible with the deceased. It becomes a matter for each pastor to decide. A Service of Naming provides a helpful alternative that can be shared with parents whose infant has been miscarried or is stillborn. I am often called to minister to parents who have experienced a miscarriage. The Service of Naming that I use includes the following elements:

Greeting or Statement of Purpose

Scripture Reading: Mark 9:33-37 or 10:13-16

Naming: (This begins with a discussion with the parents about the name that they have chosen, what it meant to them, what dreams they had for the child, the significance of having a name-identity. The naming may or may not be done with the laying-on-of-hands.)

Pastor: "A name has power. It is the sign of a person. It will represent that person to us. Her life and character will be symbolized before us by her name. A name brings with it a history. Others of us have borne that name."[10] It will link her to our life and tradition. It is by this name that we give her over into God's care.

Pastor: (To the child) You have been named _____ so you will be remembered and loved by us. By this name you are given to God to love.

Prayer.

The service is brief, but it speaks sensitively to the concern felt by parents that the event not pass unnoticed but be marked in a meaningful way.

When baptism is requested by parents, it is important to be aware of the circumstances behind the request. When an infant is ill and in danger of dying, I will gladly respond to a request for baptism. Occasionally, however, parents request baptism in the hospital for an apparently healthy infant. The belief still exists in the minds of some people that, if something should happen to their child, that infant would not be cared for by God. As already noted, the sacrament of Baptism is properly celebrated in the midst of the congregation. When this is explained to parents, I have found them to be understanding and cooperative. Where sickness threatens the life of an infant, the gathered family and hospital staff can represent the congregation. The baptism may include the following elements:

Greeting and Statement of Purpose
Invocation of God's Presence
Scripture Reading: Mark 10:13-16
Baptism
Prayer

It is important that the words and elements used to mark these rituals demonstrate awareness of the significance of the child's birth, give assurance that the child will be cared for by God (particularly important to parents who feel powerless to care for their baby), and—when death is involved—provide opportunity for parents to bond with and say good-bye to their child.

Spiritual resources help us cope with events that might otherwise overwhelm us. The pastor is uniquely trained to bring to the hospitalized patient the means whereby she can feel the support that comes from God, God's representative, and the gathered community of faith for whom that representative stands.

CHAPTER EIGHT

AFTER HOSPITALIZATION

RESOURCES WITHIN THE CONGREGATION

PASTORAL MINISTRY, including the care of those who are hospitalized, need not be carried out exclusively by the pastor. Caring for others is the ministry of the whole congregation. Howard Clinebell observes that "a local church should strive to become a healing, growth-stimulating redemptive organism. The aim of the church's pastoral care program should be to develop a dynamic climate of mutual, loving, enlightened concern, which gradually leavens the whole congregation."[1]

The development and utilization of personal resources in the congregation complements and extends the caring ministry of the pastor. Through such shared ministry more people can be touched, and care can be provided through a greater variety of and more frequent contacts. In recent decades several programs for extending and broadening the caring ministry of the church have been developed.

The Parish Nurse

The parish nurse or church nurse program of today is a recent development. It grew out of Granger Westberg's experience with church-based, holistic health care centers. Westberg is a hospital chaplain with long-term interest in the relationship of the church and health care.

The role of the Parish Nurse: A nurse in the church translates a community need into an institutional response. She [or he] is a health educator and counselor, a source for referral to community health professionals, a coordinator of volunteers and support groups, and an interpreter of the close relationship between faith and health. The role of the Parish Nurse is a constantly evolving one, ultimately defined by the needs of the congregation itself.[2]

The basic concept is relatively simple, involving the inclusion of a nurse on the church staff as a minister of holistic health care. The nurse is a partner in pastoral ministry and provides specific focus to the health care needs of the congregation and the constituency it serves.

The presence of the Parish Nurse gives people easy access to a qualified health provider, encourages people to talk about their human problems along with their "smaller" physical problems (which often indicate early cries for help), and reminds people that the church is interested in whole persons—mind, body, and spirit. The Parish Nurse functions as a member of the church staff and an extension of the pastoral role, and the Parish Nurse role develops in response to the specific needs and priorities of each congregation. Parish pastors have long seen the need for assistance as they attempt to minister to whole persons, and the partnership between the pastor and the Parish Nurse enhances the healing ministry.[3]

The parish nurse is a valuable resource in health education, programming, counseling, prevention, early screening and referral for health problems, hospital visitation, and in mobilizing the after-care of patients who are discharged from the hospital. The latter service becomes extremely important in a day of early discharge as more people must rely on home care for convalescence.

Although the Parish Nurse program began as recently as 1985, it has caught on rapidly. The development has been extensive and includes considerable diversification. Several models have emerged. These include both salaried (full-time or part-time) and volunteer parish nurses and programs jointly sponsored by hospitals and churches, as well as those sponsored exclusively by one or more churches.

The National Parish Nurse Resource Center of the Lutheran General Health Care System was established for the further development of the Parish Nurse concept. The center provides information and consultation for churches, hospitals, and other interested parties.[4]

Lay Training for Pastoral Care

Caring for one another has always been a part of congregational life. In recent decades, more programs have sprung up that carefully prepare laypersons for an informed and systematic caring ministry in the church. According to Clinebell, "Both pastors and congregations need to learn that training lay carers is not a pastor's way of passing the buck but a powerful way of deepening, broadening, and sharing the ministry of caring with the whole congregation. It does not replace pastoral care by a pastor, but rather complements and greatly augments it."[5]

One pastor devised a lay training program in pastoral care to address more adequately the need within his own congregation. This program, originally designed by Pastor Kenneth Haugk for a congregation in St. Louis, grew into the Stephen Ministries, which is now used by thousands of congregations in the United States, Canada, and throughout the world. It is probably the best-known and best-structured program available for the training of laypersons to provide an informal, caring ministry.

The Stephen Ministries is a program that equips laypeople to conduct effective caring ministry within a congregation. Congregations are enrolled in a training program of the Stephen Series, a system of training and organizing laypersons for caring ministry in and around their congregations.

Although the training programs of the Stephen Series go beyond pastoral ministry to persons with problems related to hospitalization, the focus of the Stephen Ministry is to provide a caring lay ministry to people experiencing a wide range of crisis situations, many of which are associated with hospitalization. These include ministry to the hospitalized, the terminally ill, the bereaved, the elderly, the disabled, the shut-in or institutionalized, and those continuing convalescence or rehabilitation at home. The ministry to these laypersons does not replace the pastor's ministry but complements and extends it. For example, the Stephen minister may visit a person confined to home more frequently than the pastor can and inform the pastor of special needs, supplementing the pastoral ministry.

The Stephen Ministry begins with an assessment of a congregation's needs and enrollment in the program. Following enrollment the congregation sends one or more representatives to a 12-day Leaders Training Course. The trained representative or representatives return to the congregation to recruit Stephen ministers, provide them with a minimum of fifty hours of training, and organize and implement the ministry into the continuing work of the congregation.

The Stephen Ministry is based on sound theological and psychological principles. The educational approach is thorough, precise, and well structured. It is an excellent resource for pastor and congregation to more adequately meet the needs of those who are hospitalized or who are convalescing following discharge from a hospital.[6]

RESOURCES BEYOND THE CONGREGATION

There is an almost infinite variety of services available to those with health care problems or who are in recovery. With early discharge a standard practice, there is a growing need and demand for support services and programs for recovery.

Most recovery programs focus on a specific disease, health concern, or crisis. Some are sponsored by an agency or association, while others are offered through a growing number of self-help groups. The wise pastor is knowledgeable of those services and uses them in caring for parishioners who are recovering from health-related problems. These services usually come into play during the recovery phase of treatment at the point of discharge from the hospital. In many cases the contact will be initiated by the physician or treatment team in the hospital. In those situations the pastor may wish to support the patient in following through with the recommended program of recovery. In some cases the follow through will not have been initiated, and the pastor may want to consider recommending some program of recovery. In either case it is helpful for the pastor to be familiar with the variety of resources available and the ways they may be helpful in specific situations. Most libraries have a directory of health care services. It is a useful resource of information for the pastor to keep on file.

Volunteer Health Agencies

There are a number of agencies or associations that concentrate on serving those with a specific disease. Such agencies are usually national in scope and have local or regional offices that provide a variety of services. The following national agencies offer assistance to patients and families through local chapters.

The American Cancer Society offers a variety of programs including cancer research, education, and patient services and rehabilitation to center victims. Its services include information and guidance, community health services, equipment loans for the homebound, surgical dressings, and transportation for therapy.

One program of the American Cancer Society addresses the educational and emotional needs of people with cancer. "I Can Cope" is taught in eight sessions by health care professionals in the hospitals. Its content includes learning about the disease and treatment, coping with daily health problems, expressing feelings, living with limitations, and learning about local resources.

The American Cancer Society also offers rehabilitation programs including emotional and physical support to the laryngectomy, mastectomy, and ostomy patient. Laryngectomy patients are helped by the International Association of Laryngectomies. Mastectomy patients benefit from Reach to Recovery. All three programs are similar in that they offer information and emotional support through a cadre of well-trained volunteers who have successfully adjusted to their own surgery. Upon referral from the patient's physician, the volunteers visit the patient post-operatively (pre-operatively if requested by the physician) and discuss recovery with the patient. The volunteer serves as a successful role model for the patient and provides moral support as the patient adjusts and works through recovery.

Similar programs for cancer patients are offered through other national agencies. One is the United Ostomy Association. Its membership is not limited to cancer patients, but like the American Cancer Association's programs, it offers emotional support from those with a similar experience. It is made up of local chapters of ostomates whose purpose is to provide mutual aid, support, and education to those who have had a colostomy, ileostomy, or urostomy.

The Leukemia Society of America, Inc., refers patients to local groups for emotional support. It provides consultation, information, and financial assistance for outpatient treatment for patients with leukemia and early Hodgkin's disease.

The United Cancer Council, Inc., is an association of voluntary cancer agencies that seek to control the spread of cancer through a program of service, education, and research. Direct services to cancer patients include nursing, housekeeping, medications, and prosthesis and rehabilitation services. Rehabilitation includes programs and therapy groups for colostomy, mastectomy, and laryngectomy patients and their families. Practically every major disease or handicap has a supporting voluntary health association that is similar to the American Cancer Society.[7]

Some of these agencies sponsor educational events for clergy. That is a good way to become familiar with the services offered by the agency as well as a good avenue to understanding the struggles of persons suffering with different diseases.

Self-Help or Support Groups

There are a growing number of self-help groups. Many of the agencies just mentioned sponsor self-help groups that are appropriate to the agencies' specific purpose. There are other self-help groups that are not affiliated with a particular agency and have come into existence in order to address specific needs of people with common health-related problems.

The prime example of such self-help groups is Alcoholics Anonymous with its concentration on those in lifelong recovery from alcoholism. Its approach has been extended to families of alcoholics through the programs of Al-Anon and Alateens.

That Alcoholics Anonymous' spiritually-oriented 12-step program has been adopted by so many groups is testimony to its phenomenal effectiveness in the recovery from addictive disorders. Its approach has been adapted by Narcotics Anonymous, Families Anonymous, Gamblers Anonymous, Overeaters Anonymous, and others. The pastor can become familiar with this approach to recovery through reading and attending the groups' open meetings. They are the pastor's best resource in supporting people in recovery from addictive disorders.

There are self-help groups that focus on other diseases that are not addictive in nature. Most of these do not use the 12-step approach of A.A. Some, such as Recovery Incorporated, are mental health oriented. There is a group for patients recovering from eating disorders (anorexia nervosa and bulimia).

Contrasting with self-help groups whose purpose is that of helping people in the recovery from various diseases are those that help people through bereavement. Bereavement may be due to the actual death of a loved one or the anticipatory grief over a person who is terminally ill. In either case the grief is often associated with hospitalization and is closely connected to the pastor's hospital ministry.

One such group, Make Today Count, was formed for terminally ill patients and their families. It grew out of the experience of Orville Kelly, who was terminally ill himself. He and his wife found that they were poorly prepared to cope with his life-threatening illness. Out of their experience they formed a peer support group for people with a life-threatening illness. Its singular goal is "living each day as fully and completely as possible." Its membership includes patients with a life-threatening disease, their families, nurses, physicians, other health care professionals, and interested community members.

One organization for bereaved parents is international in scope. The Compassionate Friends has local mutual support groups. There are even special groups for parents who have lost a child through suicide. Local hospitals can provide information about such groups.

Often grief groups are sponsored locally by hospitals and other institutions. In some larger congregations it is possible to organize grief groups for the recently bereaved or groups specifically for the recently widowed. Many full-service congregations are character-ized by the vast numbers of support groups that are available to members and to the community, so that attendance throughout the week is often greater than on Sunday morning.

The programs described in this chapter provide a broad but by no means exhaustive sample of resources that are available to supplement the pastoral ministry to the hospitalized parishioner. They vary from congregation-based services to those that are provided by the larger community and are available to the general public. The congregation-based programs require primary effort, responsibility, and some funding on the part of the congregation. The parish nurse program may require the addition of a professional staff member while the Stephen Ministry requires a serious commitment to lay education and participation. The larger community programs such as voluntary agencies and self-help groups require some pastoral awareness. They provide valuable resources that can be appropriated by individuals and their families. They may be used to augment the caring ministry of the pastor and church.

CHAPTER NINE

THE PASTORAL VISIT

THE PASTORAL visit goes beyond a social visit in that the role and function of the pastor are activated. A pastoral call is made with a specific purpose. Such a purpose gives the visit focus, and the visit becomes more meaningful. Without purpose, pastoral visits can fall into an aimless routine and become an obligatory pastime.

Having a professional purpose does not mean that the pastor should push a predetermined agenda. The anticipated purpose of a visit may prove to be mistaken and need to be modified. A parallel to this process in the hospital setting is that every patient is admitted with a diagnosis. That diagnosis is used to determine where and in which service the patient is to be placed. Further differential diagnosis may confirm the admitting diagnosis or suggest that the diagnosis be altered.

The purpose of any pastoral visit is to discern the need of the person or persons being visited and to respond appropriately to the need. To some degree, the pastor can anticipate the need from the information provided and what is known of the person to be visited. Need is determined by an educated guess. Upon further assessment, an anticipatory impression may or may not prove valid.

An example from recent experience will illustrate how

anticipatory impressions function and may have to be adjusted. A teen-aged boy who had suffered a severe head trauma was admitted to the emergency room. His mother arrived soon after. She was alone and said that her husband, the boy's father, was on his way. When she asked to see her son, the doctor hesitated and said she would need to wait for a while. The doctor, the nurse, and I agreed that it would be best if we delayed until her husband arrived so that they could support each other. Her son's face was badly lacerated and his head was swollen. When her husband arrived he was overwhelmed and could not bring himself to see his son. She went in to be with her son and offered emotional support to her husband. Our expectations proved to be unfounded, and I had to adjust my initial impressions.

At its best, the pastoral visit is a caring dialogue of prayer. It is a conversation in which the Holy Spirit participates, both in the hearing and the speaking, and brings about understanding. ''For where two or three are gathered in my name, I am there among them'' (Matthew 18:20). When the visit is truly pastoral, the caring grace of God is realized through the medium of conversation.

Elias Porter, a psychologist, identified five categories of responses used in counseling. These five responses are applicable to pastoral conversation. They are useful in examining the pastoral visit. The five responses are:

E—Evaluative. A response which indicates the pastor has made a judgment of relative goodness, appropriateness, effectiveness, and rightness. The response implies what the parishioner might or ought to do, explicitly or implicitly.

I—Interpretive. A response which indicates that the pastor's intent is to teach, to impart meaning to the parishioner, to show something. This response suggests, obviously or subtly, what the parishioner might or ought to think.

S—Supportive. A response which indicates that the pastor's intent is to reassure, to reduce the parishioner's intensity of feeling, to pacify. It implies that the parishioner ought not to feel as she does.

P—Probing. A response which indicates that the pastor's intent is to seek further information, to provoke further discussion along a certain line, to query. It implies that the person ought to or might profitably develop or discuss a point further. Most probes are in the form of questions.

U—Understanding. A response which indicates that the pastor's intent is to so respond as in effect to ask the person whether the counselor understands accurately what he is "saying," how he "feels" about it, how it "strikes" him, how he "sees" it. Understanding may be related to content or to the feeling. Responses to feelings are most likely to be empathic. They are hearing with what Theodore Reik called the "third ear."[1]

Put in other terms, an evaluative response is one that carries the pastor's value judgment; an interpretive response is one that intends to teach or explain the dynamics of a person's behavior (the "why"); a supportive response is one that seeks to reassure, inspire, or undergird a person; a probing response is one that questions; and an understanding response is one that reflects the pastor's feelings, attitudes, and thoughts.

The EISPU categories are very useful in helping pastors and students to become aware of lopsidedness existing in their communication. The pastoral visits of many parish ministers consist almost entirely of P (probing) and S (supportive) responses, without their being aware of it. Moralistic ministers tend to major in E (evaluative) and P (probing) responses. Pastors who have some knowledge of psychodynamic theory often emphasize I (interpretive) responses, demonstrating their theories about why people feel and act as they do. Those whose only training has been in the Rogerian approach to counseling may rely excessively on U (understanding) responses. Ministers with no training in counseling and pastoral care seldom use U or reflective responses.[2]

All five categories of responses have a valid place in pastoral conversation. A minister should be able to use them all with flexible selectivity, depending on the needs of the particular counseling relationship. The key is to use them appropriately.

The usefulness of the EISPUA system is enhanced if two types of P responses are distinguished—PI (probing for information) and PF (probing for feelings). The system is a valuable tool for analyzing written verbatim reports or recorded counseling tapes, helping to identify the blindspots in the counselor's responses.[3]

The EISPU categories are used in examining the following pastoral conversation. The conversation is rather typical of a visit with a hospitalized parishioner.

The patient is a sixty-two-year-old, married man. He was a senior vice president in an engineering firm. Six months prior to his present hospitalization he had back surgery, which resulted in paraplegia. The current hospitalization is for the treatment of a decubitus (bed sore) at the base of his spine. The patient has become septic (infected).

Pastor Kirk has talked with the charge nurse and has learned that the patient, Mr. Joe Bridgeman, is discouraged, apparently depressed, and has no appetite. Although his paraplegia will remain, he can expect a full recovery from his decubitus and sepsis. His recovery is impeded by his lack of motivation and lack of nourishment.

Pastor Kirk's task is to make an immediate assessment of Mr. Bridgeman's needs and determine and employ an appropriate pastoral response. If the pastoral diagnosis is consistent with the information just given, the pastoral purpose might be to assist Mr. Bridgeman in mobilizing his faith or spiritual resources for recovery. An appropriate pastoral response will emerge from attentive, empathic listening that seeks first to understand the patient. It will be important to hear his perception of his situation. Does he view himself as a helpless victim or does he perceive that he can claim some responsibility for his own recovery?

Pastor Kirk enters the patient's room, silently praying for a sense of God's presence. The patient is in the bed by the window. A curtain is halfway drawn between the two beds in the room. A woman is at the bedside of the other patient. Mrs. Bridgeman is sitting in a chair at the foot of her husband's bed. She is reading a magazine and not talking to her husband as the pastor enters. Joe is emaciated and is on a special air bed with some tubes connected to an apparatus at his bedside. He is watching television.

P.1 Pastor: Hello, Mary (to Mrs. Bridgeman). Hello Joe. (There are no other chairs in the rather crowded room so pastor Kirk stands near the head of Joe's bed facing both Joe and his wife sitting at the foot of the bed.)

M.1 Mary: Hello, Pastor. I'm glad you came to see Joe. (**May suggest she is losing patience with Joe.**)

P.2 Pastor: Thanks for letting me know he was back in the hospital. How is it going with you Joe? (**Open-ended probe**)

J.2 Joe: (Turning down the volume on the TV set) Oh, not very good. Terrible.

P.3 Pastor: You have really had a rough time of it during the past year. (**Understanding response that reflects Joe's statement in J.2. It conveys understanding and usually evokes candor.**)

J.3 Joe: Yes, it has been a real nightmare. I come out of the surgery paralyzed. They said it rarely happens, but that is small comfort when it happens to you. I was just getting into my rehabilitation and then I got this bedsore from sitting in my wheelchair. Now that is infected and it isn't healing. We don't seem to be getting anywhere. Sometimes I think they don't know what they are doing around here.

P.4 Pastor: You are in a good place here Joe. This hospital has an excellent reputation. If anyone can help you get well, these people can. (**Supportive response. While the pastor's intent is to reassure, the implication is that Joe should not feel as he does. Joe is apt to feel that he is not understood and his feelings are not acceptable. This could result in Joe's becoming more guarded in his statements.**)

J.4 Joe: Well, a lot of people are interested in me O.K. They come in to examine me; ask a lot of questions.

Everybody analyzes me. They say I am depressed. So this morning they sent a psychiatrist in to talk to me. **(Hints at Joe's reaction to being treated as an object. It is a signal to the pastor to steer clear of a problem-solving approach and relate to Joe more personally.)**

P.5 Pastor: It sounds as though you resent a lot of the attention that is being focused on you. I guess you feel like a guinea pig. **(Is an Interpretive remark. It explains Joe's feelings. The interpretation may or may not be accurate. Joe may confirm or deny the interpretation. He also may become more cautious and evasive as he senses he is being analyzed by the pastor.)**

J.5 Joe: Well, *I* know I'm depressed. I don't need any expert to tell me that. Everybody is trying to get me to eat. They say I can't heal until I eat. If I won't eat they are going to put in a feeding tube. Well I can't eat if I don't feel like it. I just don't have any appetite.

P.6 Pastor: You feel pushed. **(Understanding response)**

J.6 Joe: Well, I am being pushed. I know they mean well but I just don't care anymore. What's the use? I lived a decent life. I never did anything to hurt anybody. I did things to help others. We were making plans to enjoy retirement and then this. **(Here is the ultimate theological challenge. If God is good, and all powerful, why do terrible things happen to good people?)**

P.7 Pastor: It seems as if even God has let you down. **(The challenge in J.6 can tempt the pastor to respond in several ways. One of those is to respond intellectually and give rational, theological, philosophical answers to the dilemma. One might even be tempted to launch into an exposition of Job. What is needed is a compassionate, understanding response, which accepts the feelings and supports the person in the faith struggle.)**

J.7 Joe: That's right. I don't know whether just to damn God or simply realize I don't have any control anyway. If God has any control he sure has screwed me up.

P.8 Pastor: Your anger with God places you in good company with those who have struggled with their faith. The psalmists questioned God and said things like, "Good Lord where are you? Why have you abandoned me? How long will you turn your face from me?" I believe it is good to let God know how you feel; that God can hear the prayer of your anger. **(Is primarily evaluative. The pastor grows a little sermonic here. There is an attempt to convey acceptance of the dilemma and the struggle. There is also an attempt to use scripture dialogically and connect Joe's struggle with faith with similar struggles of biblical figures. It at least blesses the struggle and does not dismiss it.)**

J.8 Joe: It seems everybody wants something from me. My mother calls me from Bay City and says when are you going to get well so you can come and take care of me?

P.9 Pastor: Does anybody care for you just for who you are and not for what you do? **(Probe)**

J.9 Joe: (Pointing at wife) Her. She has stood by me through everything.

P.10 Pastor: So there is at least one person who cares for you for yourself.

J.10 Joe: Yes. And there is Joey too.

P.11 Pastor: Joey? **(Probe for information)**

J.11 Joe: Yes. He is my grandson. (Joe smiles and his eyes brighten.) He was named after me. He is special.

P.12 Pastor: I can tell.

J.12 Joe: This is his first day at school. I've been trying to get him on the phone. If I weren't stuck in here I would be with him. Now I don't know how much I'm going to be able to do. A lot that I looked forward to will never be.

P.13 Pastor: You really miss Joey. **(Understanding)**

J.13 Joe: Yes, don't think there is any future in this. I just want to go. **(Pastor is not sure what he means. It is better to ask than to make assumptions. A probe is in order.)**

P.14 Pastor: Go where? **(Probe for clarification)**

J.14 Joe: (Emphatically) Die. (Long pause)

P.15 Pastor: You would rather die because of the paralysis? **(Probe for clarification)**

J.15 Joe: No, I can live with that. I could get around in a wheelchair. We were handling that O.K. But this never feeling good, being confined in bed; I just can't take it.

P.16 Pastor: It's going to take some time Joe. But you're going to get better. **(Supportive response again attempts to reassure. But premature and shallow reassurance fails to take Joe's feeling seriously.)**

J.16 Joe: Well, I don't know about that. I'm *not* getting any better. Things just go from bad to worse.

P.17 Pastor: You don't feel very hopeful. **(Understanding response. Recognizes the attempt to reassure is not going anywhere.)**

J.17 Joe: No, I don't.

P.18 Pastor: Joe, I believe that nothing can separate us from the love of God. I know it does not feel that way to you right now Joe. But my prayer is that you will experience God's presence with you even in your present despair; that God will strengthen you for the living of these days and grant you comfort and peace. **(Has elements of supportive and understanding responses. Here the supportive responses are more realistic and do not minimize or discount what Joe feels.)**

J.18 Joe: Thanks for coming to see me pastor. I do appreciate it.

M.18 Mary: Yes, Pastor Kirk, thanks for visiting with Joe.

P.19 Pastor: Maybe you can get that call through to Joey now.

I'm sure he would like to tell his grandpa what his day has been like. He must be missing you too. **(Evaluative, as it suggests what Joe should do.)**

J.19 Joe: Yes, I am going to call him now.

P.20 Pastor: Very good, Joe. I'm glad I got to visit with you today. Goodbye, Mary. I'll see you and Joe again in a couple of days. **(Evaluative)**

This visit presents the pastor with a challenging situation. It calls for a response that could include all three pastoral functions: guiding, healing, and sustaining. The temptation for some pastors would be to respond exclusively in terms of a healing approach. That could lead to an over-reliance on reassurance and an unrealistic attempt to "fix" Joe's situation. The result might well be an increased feeling of frustration and alienation for Joe. Certainly some healing of spirit and attitude is appropriate in this case, and the pastor would want to support it. The pastor did highlight the relationships that contribute to Joe's investment in life.

In pastoral exchanges 8 and 18, the pastor makes reference to scriptures that reflect an understanding of the despair Joe is currently experiencing and expressing. This demonstrates an empathic use of scripture rather than a judgmental one. This use of scripture conveys an acceptance of his struggle and implies a hope beyond the struggle without insisting he get to that point immediately.

In similar fashion the prayer in the 18th exchange suggests both understanding and hope. It also demonstrates an appreciation of the dialogue between pastor and person as a form of prayer in itself. The more traditional form of addressing the prayer directly to God would have been intrusive given Joe's anger at God at this time. This approach communicates sensitivity to Joe's feelings. The principle of this approach to prayer is similar to that invoked by Jesus in the story of the raising of Lazarus. After he had prayed in the presence of the people, he said to God, "I knew that you always hear me, but I have said this for the sake of the crowd standing here, so that they may believe that you sent me" (John 11:42).

On other occasions, of course, the more formal, traditional prayer would certainly be appropriate. The setting and situation need to be considered.

In any pastoral conversation there are an infinite variety of possibilities. There is no single right way to respond. However some responses are more effective than others and convey understanding and acceptance. When that happens there is evidence that the grace of God is at work in the interchange between pastor and parishioner. Real sustaining, guiding, and healing occur, and the loving care of God becomes incarnate. Persons experience divine grace and healing, and God is glorified.

NOTES

1. A PASTORAL THEOLOGY

1. Henri Nouwen, *The Living Reminder: Service and Prayer in the Memory of Jesus Christ* (New York: Seabury Press, 1977).
2. Leroy Aden and J. Harold Ellens, eds., *The Church and Pastoral Care* (Grand Rapids: Baker Book House, 1988), p. 59. Relationships are reviewed as having an inherently sacramental quality.
3. Ibid., p. 63.
4. Paul Tillich, "The Theology of Pastoral Care" in *Pastoral Psychology* 10 (October 1959): 21-26.
5. Martin Luther, *Letters of Spiritual Counsel*, ed. and trans. Theodore G. Tappert, *Library of Christian Classics*, vol. 18 (Philadelphia: Westminster Press, 1955), p. 27.
6. Seward Hiltner, *Preface to Pastoral Theology* (Nashville/New York: Abingdon Press, 1958), p. 68.
7. Ibid., p. 69.
8. Nouwen, *The Living Reminder*, p. 26.
9. Hiltner, *Preface to Pastoral Theology*, p. 116.
10. Ibid., p. 146.

2. THE HOSPITAL COMMUNITY

1. Will Durant, *The Story of Civilization: Part 4—The Age of Faith* (New York: Simon and Schuster, 1950), p. 77.
2. Ronald L. Numbers and Darrel W. Amundsen, eds., *Caring and Curing: Health and Medicine in the Western Religious Traditions* (New York: Macmillan, 1986), p. 49.
3. Will Durant, *The Age of Faith*, p. 78.
4. Oration 20, Quoted in W. Smith and S. Cheetham, *A Dictionary of Christian Antiquities, Vol. 1* (London, 1875), s.v. "Hospitals," p. 786.
5. Numbers and Amundsen, *Caring and Curing*, p. 3.
6. James B. Nelson, *Human Medicine: Ethical Perspectives on New Medical Issues* (Minneapolis: Augsburg Publishing House, 1973), p. 28.

3. THE PASTOR'S HOMEWORK

1. *Existential Psychotherapy* (New York: Basic Books, 1980), p. 96.
2. Reinhold Niebuhr, *Justice and Mercy,* ed. Ursula M. Niebuhr (New York: Harper, 1974), pp. 15, 16, 20.
3. Ibid., p. 20.
4. *The Wounded Healer* (New York: Doubleday Image Books, 1979), p. xvi.
5. Nathan A. Scott, "The Burdens and Temptations of the Pulpit," in *Preaching on Suffering and a God of Love,* ed. and with a foreword by Henry J. Young (Philadelphia: Fortress Press, 1978), p. 7.
6. These approaches are discussed in depth in Kent D. Richmond, *Preaching to Sufferers: God and the Problem of Pain* (Nashville: Abingdon Press, 1988).
7. Dorothee Soelle, *Suffering,* trans. Everett Kalin (Philadelphia: Fortress Press, 1975), p. 114.
8. S. Paul Schilling, *God and Human Anguish* (Nashville: Abingdon Press, 1977), p. 203.
9. *See,* e.g., David R. Griffin, "Creation Out of Chaos and the Problem of Evil," in *Encountering Evil,* ed. Stephen T. David (Atlanta: John Knox Press, 1981), p. 76.
10. Daniel Day Williams, "The Vulnerable and the Invulnerable God," *Christianity and Crisis* 22 (March 5, 1962): 28.
11. *See,* e.g., Ernest Becker, *The Denial of Death* (New York: Free Press, 1973).
12. *Pilgrim at Tinker Creek* (New York: Bantam Books, 1974).
13. *Death: The Final Stage of Growth* (Englewood Cliffs, N.J.: Prentice-Hall, 1975), p. 145.
14. *Existential Psychotherapy,* p. 40.
15. Kübler-Ross, *Death,* p. 26.

4. THE PASTOR'S BIO-ETHICS

1. "The Beginnings of Personhood: Theological Considerations," in *Moral Medicine: Theological Perspectives in Medical Ethics* (Grand Rapids, Mich.: Wm. B. Eerdman's Publishing Co., 1987), p. 393.
2. *The Book of Discipline of the United Methodist Church* (Nashville: Abingdon Press, 1984), p. 91.
3. Sidney Wanzer, et al., "The Physician's Responsibility Toward Hopelessly Ill Patients," *The New England Journal of Medicine* 310 (no. 15): 957.
4. The 10 percent figure was cited by a physician at a medical-ethical lecture attended by the authors. *See also* Judith Wilson Ross, Deborah Pugh, "Limited Cardiopulmonary Resuscitation: The Ethics of Partial Codes," in *Quality Review Bulletin* (January 1988), pp. 4-8.
5. David L. Schiedermayer, "Can Doctors Agree with God on the Time to Die?" *Christian Medical Society Journal* 17 (Summer 1986): 15.
6. *Guidelines on the Termination of Life-Sustaining Treatment and the Care of the Dying* (Bloomington, Ind.: Indiana University Press, 1987), p. 5.
7. George J. Annas, "Do Feeding Tubes Have More Rights Than Patients?" *The Hastings Center Report* (February 1986), p. 26.
8. *See,* e.g., Stephen E. Lammers and Allen Verhey, *On Moral Medicine: Theological Perspectives in Medical Ethics* (Grand Rapids, Mich.: Wm. B. Eerdman's Publishing Co., 1987).
9. Joanne Lynn and James F. Childress, "Must Patients Always Be Given Food and Water?" *The Hastings Center Report* 13 (October 1983): 20. *See also* Council on Scientific Affairs and Council on Ethical and Judicial Affairs, "Persistent Vegetative

State and the Decision to Withdraw or Withhold Life Support'' *JAMA* 263 (January 19, 1990): 426-30; and, Laurel Arthur Burton, ''An Interview with Ronald E. Cranford,'' *The Care Giver Journal* 7 (no. 3, 1990): 5-14. Journal of the College of Chaplains, A Division of the American Protestant Health Association, 1701 Woodfield Rd., Suite 311, Schaumburg, IL.

10. Pope John Paul II, ''On Euthanasia,'' in Lammers and Verhey, *On Moral Medicine*, p. 442.

11. Allan L. Otten, ''Can't We Put My Mother To Sleep?'' *The Wall Street Journal*, Wednesday, June 5, 1985.

12. P.O. Box 11830, Eugene, OR. An excellent recent treatment of the subject can be found in *Active Euthanasia, Religion and the Public Debate*, The Park Ridge Center, 676 N. St. Clair, Suite 450, Chicago, IL.

6. THE PATIENT'S NEEDS

1. (Grand Rapids, Mich.: Wm. B. Eerdman's Publishing Co., 1990), pp. 81ff.

2. *See*, e.g., Armando Parces Enriquez, ed., *People in Crisis: Understanding and Helping* (Redwood City, Calif.: Addison-Wesley Publishing Co., 1989); Charles V. Gerkin, *Crisis Experience in Modern Life* (Nashville: Abingdon, 1979); Harvey D. Grant, et al., *Emergency Care* (Englewood Cliffs, N.J.: Prentice-Hall, 1986).

3. Robert R. Kirby, Joseph M. Civetta, and Robert W. Taylor, eds., *Introduction to Critical Care* (Philadelphia: J. B. Lippincott, 1989), p. 210.

4. *In Memoriam* (Notre Dame, Ind.: Ave Maria Press, 1980), p. 14.

5. Linda L. LaMontagne, ''Children's Preoperative Coping: Replication and Extension,'' *Nursing Research* 36 (May-June 1987): 166ff.

6. John E. Sarno, Martha Taylor Sarno, with an Intro. by Howard A. Rusk, *Stroke: A Guide for Patients and Their Families* (New York: McGraw-Hill, 1979), p. 124.

7. *See* Alquinn S. Toews, ''A Ministry to the Unconscious Patient,'' in Richard Dayringer, ed., *Pastor and Patient* (New York: Jason Aaronson and Son, 1981), pp. 178-83.

8. ''AIDS Marks Tenth Anniversary,'' in *The Kenosha News*, June 10, 1991, p. 15, from an article by B. D. Cohen in *Newsday*.

9. (New York: Macmillan, 1969).

10. The following stages are taken from Heather George's presentation in ''Counseling People with AIDS, Their Lovers, Friends, and Relations,'' in John Green, Alana McCreaner, eds., *Counseling in HIV Infection and Aids* (Oxford: Blackwell Scientific Publications, 1989), pp. 69-87.

11. Robert J. Marx, ''Choose the Blessing,'' in *Pastoral Care and Cancer*, The American Cancer Society, publication PE #132, pp. 17-19.

7. THE PASTOR'S SPIRITUAL RESOURCES

1. *The Minister As Diagnostician* (Philadelphia: Westminster Press, 1976): *See esp.* chap. 4, pp. 44-60.

2. *See*, e.g., Norman Cousins, *Anatomy of an Illness* (Toronto: Bantam Books, 1979) and Bernie S. Siegel, *Love, Medicine, and Miracles* (New York: Harper and Row, 1986).

3. *The Cardiac Patient* (Minneapolis: Augsburg, 1978). *See esp.* pp. 97ff.

4. Kenneth R. Mitchell, ''Ritual in Pastoral Care,'' *The Journal of Pastoral Care* 43 (Spring 1989): 74.

5. *See*, e.g., Perry H. Biddle, Jr., *Abingdon Hospital Visitation Manual* (Nashville: Abingdon Press, 1988), pp. 183ff.

6. (Nashville: Abingdon, 1976), pp. 53ff.
7. *The Embodied Word* (Minneapolis: Fortress Press, 1991), p. 52.
8. Copies can be ordered from
   The Upper Room
   1908 Grand Avenue
   P.O. Box 189
   Nashville, TN 37202.
9. "Ritual in Pastoral Care," in *The Journal of Pastoral Care* 43 (Spring 1989): 73.
10. *Ritual in a New Day,* p. 48.

8. AFTER HOSPITALIZATION

1. Howard Clinebell, *Basic Types of Pastoral Care & Counseling: Resources for the Ministry of Healing and Growth,* rev. and enlarged (Nashville: Abingdon Press, 1984), p. 395.
2. Anne Marie Djupe, Harriet Olson, Judith Ryan, and Jan Lantz, *Reaching Out, Parish Nursing Services* (Park Ridge, Ill.: National Parish Resource Center, a division of Lutheran General Health Care System, 1991), from Introduction.
3. Ibid., p. 3.
4. The address is 1775 Dempster Street, Park Ridge, IL 60068-1174.
5. Clinebell, *Basic Types of Pastoral Care & Counseling,* p. 397.
6. For more information regarding the Stephen Ministries, correspondence may be addressed to: Stephen Ministries, 1325 Boland, St. Louis, MO 63117. The phone number is 314/645-5511.
7. See appendix B for a listing of some of these agencies.

9. THE PASTORAL VISIT

1. Adapted from Elias H. Porter, *An Introduction to Therapeutic Counseling* (Boston: Houghton Mifflin, 1950), p. 201.
2. Howard Clinebell, *Basic Types of Pastoral Care & Counseling: Resources for the Ministry of Healing and Growth,* rev. and enlarged (Nashville: Abingdon Press, 1984), p. 95.
3. Ibid., p. 96. Clinebell added the A category in his most recent edition of *Basic Types of Pastoral Care & Counseling.* It was not one of the original categories and is not germane to the purpose of this chapter.

APPENDIX A

_-_._._-_._-_

A HELP AND GUIDANCE
In the Event of My Death

Name _____ Telephone No. _____

Home Address _____ City _____

Date of Birth _____ Place of Birth _____

Social Security Number _____

Nearest of Kin (other than immediate family)

1. Name _____ Relationship _____

Phone _____

Address _____ City _____ State _____

2. Name _____ Relationship _____

Phone _____

Address _____ City _____ State _____

It is acknowledged that the information and instructions provided in this questionnaire are for the guidance of my family and friends in making the arrangements necessary at the time of my death and are not legally binding or enforceable.

I hereby give the following instructions: (It is not necessary to answer all questions completely, only those which apply to you.)

1. ____ I wish that my body or parts thereof (state which) be used for medical purposes. (Provisions have been made by proper documentation in accordance with _____.)

2. ____ A. I desire the following mortuary to handle my affairs:

Name _____ City _____ State _____

If above out of town, local mortuary name _____

B. I wish cremation, with disposition as follows:

Ashes to be buried: Place _____

City _____ State _____

APPENDIX A

Ashes to be placed in depository as follows:

Place _____

City _____   State _____

C. I wish burial in a casket.

Place of burial _____

City _____   State _____

Casket desired:

Least expensive__ Moderately expensive__ Most expensive __

Type of Plot: Ground _____ Crypt _____

Already purchased? __ If so, where:

Place _____

_____

City _____   State _____

3. _____ I wish the following memorial service:

APPENDIX A

A. If you have any text preferences for your memorial service, you

   may indicate it here: _____

   _____

   _____

B. Place of service: Church ____ Funeral home ____

   Name _____

   City _____   State _____

C. Body to be viewed? Yes ____ No ____

D. Flowers desired? Yes ____ No ____

E. Desire embalming? Yes ____ No ____

F. I desire the committal services to be conducted at: (Check one)

   ____ 1. In conjunction with the memorial service at either the
           church or funeral home.

   ____ 2. At the gravesite, mausoleum, or crematory.

   ____ 3. At the discretion of the funeral director, clergyperson, or
           family.

G. Organizations participating:

Name _____

Name _____

H. Miscellaneous

Organist: _____

Choir or Soloist: _____
Musical selections:

_____

_____

_____

4. ____ Memorial gifts to following organizations:

A. Name _____

Address _____ City _____

State _____

B. Name_____

   Address _____ City _____

   State _____

C. Name _____

   Address _____ City _____

   State _____

5. ____ Do you have a will? Yes ____ No ____

   A. Location of Will: _____

   B. Name of Attorney: _____

   City _____ State _____

6. ____ If you have any other instructions or requests not included above,

   please indicate here: _____

   _____

   _____

   _____

   _____

   _____.

Note: If you need any help with this questionnaire, feel free to call the church office.

APPENDIX B

SUPPORT AGENCIES

AIDS—1-800-AID-AIDS

Addiction: Alcoholics Anonymous—312-346-1475

Gamblers Anonymous—312-346-1588

Alzheimer's Disease: 312-361-4500 ext. 5061

Arthritis: The National Arthritis Foundation—1-800-572-2397

Burns—The National Burn Victim Foundation, 308 Main Street, Orange, NJ 07050

Cancer: The American Cancer Society, National Headquarters, 777 Third Avenue, New York, NY 10017, 212-371-2900

The National Hospice Org., 301 Tower Suite 506, 301 Maple Avenue West, Vienna, VA 22180

Make Today Count, P.O. Box 303, Burlington, IA 52601

Cystic Fibrosis—1-800-824-5064

Diabetes: The American Diabetes Association, 312-346-1805

Eating Disorders: National Association of Anorexia Nervosa and Associated Disorders—312-831-3438
Overeaters Anonymous: 312-922-7676

Epilepsy: Epilepsy Foundation of America, 4351 Garden City Drive, Landover, MD 20785

APPENDIX B

Heart Disease: The American Heart Association: 312-346-4675

Hypoglycemia: The National Hypoglycemia Association, P.O. Box 120, Ridgewood, NJ 07451

Kidney Disease: The National Kidney Foundation 312-663-3103

Leukemia: The Leukemia Society of America, Inc., 211 East 43rd Street, New York, NY 10017, 212-573-8484

Liver Disease: The American Liver Foundation
National Headquarters, 1425 Pompton Avenue, Cedar Grove, NJ 07009

Multiple Sclerosis: 1-800-922-0484

Muscular Dystrophy: 312-986-8450

Myasthenia Gravis: 1-800-888-6208

Organ Transplant or Donation: United Network for Organ Sharing
Organ Donation Hotline, 1100 Boulder Parkway; Suite 500, Richmond, VA 23225

Ostomy: The United Ostomy Association, Inc., 1111 Wilshire Boulevard, Los Angeles, CA 90017, 213-481-2811

Parkinson's Disease: American Parkinson's Disease Association, 116 John Street, New York, NY 10038

National Parkinson's Foundation, 1501 NW 9th Avenue, Miami, FL 33136

Sickle Cell Anemia: The National Association for Sickle Cell Diseases, Inc., 4221 Wilshire Boulevard, Los Angeles, CA 90010

Spina Bifida: Spinal Bifida Association of America, 1700 Rockville Pike #540, Rockville, MD 20852

Suicide: The American Association of Suicidology, 2459 S. Ash, Denver, CO 80222

BIBLIOGRAPHY

BOOKS

A Service of Death and Resurrection: The Ministry of the Church at Death, Supplemental Worship Resources 7. Nashville: Abingdon, 1979.

Active Euthanasia, Religion and the Public Debate. The Park Ridge Center, 676 N. St. Clair; Suite 450; Chicago, IL.

Aden, Leroy, and J. Harold Ellens, eds. *The Church and Pastoral Care.* Grand Rapids, Mich.: Baker Book House, 1988.

Aguilera, Donna C. *Crisis Intervention: Theory and Methodology.* St. Louis, Mo.: C. V. Mosby Co., 1990.

Banks, Herman J., and Anne T. Romano. *Human Relations for Emergency Response Personnel.* Springfield, Ill.: Charles C. Thomas, 1982.

Biddle, Perry H., Jr. *Abingdon Hospital Visitation Manual.* Nashville: Abingdon Press, 1988.

Blanchet, Kevin D., ed. *AIDS: A Healthcare Management Response.* Rockville, Md.: Aspen Publications, 1988.

Buber, Martin. *I and Thou.* Trans. Ronald Gregor Smith. New York: Charles Scribner's Sons, 1958.

Burgess, Ann Wolbert, and Bruce A. Baldwin. *Crisis Intervention Theory and Practice: A Clinical Handbook.* Englewood Cliffs, N.J.: Prentice-Hall, 1982.

Clinebell, Howard. *Basic Types of Pastoral Care & Counseling: Resources for the Ministry of Healing and Growth,* rev. and enlarged. Nashville: Abingdon Press, 1984.

Cousins, Norman. *Anatomy of an Illness.* Toronto: Bantam Books, 1979.

Dayringer, Richard, ed. *Pastor and Patient.* New York: Jason Aaronson and Son, 1981.

Dixon, Samuel L. *Working with People in Crisis: Theory and Practice.* St. Louis, Mo.: C. V. Mosby Co., 1979.

Enriquez, Armando Parces, ed. *People in Crisis: Understanding and Helping.* Redwood City, Calif.: Addison-Wesley Publishing Co., 1989.

BIBLIOGRAPHY

Franklyn, Mary Beth. *After Pregnancy Loss*. Discipleship Resources. Nashville: Abingdon Press, 1988.

Gerkin, Charles V. *Crisis Experience in Modern Life*. Nashville: Abingdon, 1979.

Grant, Harvey D., et al. *Emergency Care*. Englewood Cliffs, N.J.: Prentice-Hall, 1986.

Green, John, and Alana McCreaner, eds. *Counseling in HIV Infection and AIDS*. Oxford: Blackwell Scientific Publications, 1989.

Guidelines on the Termination of Life-Sustaining Treatment and the Care of the Dying. A report by the Hastings Center. Bloomington, Ind.: Indiana University Press, 1987.

Hafen, Brent Q., and Keith J. Karren, eds. *Pre-Hospital Emergency Care and Crisis Intervention*. Englewood, Col.: Morton Publishing Co., 1981.

Hafen, Brent Q., and Brenda Peterson, with Kathryn J. Frandsen. *The Crisis Intervention Handbook*. Englewood Cliffs, N.J.: Prentice-Hall, 1982.

Hauerwas, Stanley. *Naming the Silences*. Grand Rapids, Mich.: Wm. B. Eerdman's Publishing Co., 1990.

Hiltner, Seward. *Preface to Pastoral Theology*. Nashville/New York: Abingdon Press, 1958.

Hipple, John L., and Lee B. Hipple. *Diagnosis and Management of Psychological Emergencies*. Springfield, Ill.: Charles C. Thomas, 1983.

Hoff, Lee Ann. *People in Crisis: Understanding and Helping*. Redwood City, Calif.: Addison-Wesley, 1989.

Holst, Lawrence E., ed., with Introduction by Martin E. Martin. *Hospital Ministry: The Role of the Chaplain Today*. New York: Crossroad, 1985.

Humphrey, Derek. *Let Me Die Before I Wake*. Eugene, Oreg.: Hemlock Society, 1984.

Kirby, Robert R., Joseph M. Civetta, and Robert W. Taylor, eds. *Introduction to Critical Care*. Philadelphia: J. B. Lippincott, 1989.

Lammers, Stephen E., and Allen Verhey. *On Moral Medicine: Theological Perspectives in Medical Ethics*. Grand Rapids, Mich.: Wm. B. Eerdman's Publishing Co., 1987.

Luther, Martin. *Letters of Spiritual Counsel*. Ed. and trans. Theodore G. Tappert. *Library of Christian Classics*, vol. 18. Philadelphia: Westminster Press, 1955.

Mitchell, Kenneth R. *Hospital Chaplain*. Philadelphia: Westminster Press, 1972.

Nelson, James B. *Human Medicine: Ethical Perspectives on New Medical Issues*. Minneapolis: Augsburg Publishing House, 1973.

Nouwen, Henri. *The Living Reminder: Service and Prayer in the Memory of Jesus Christ*. New York: Seabury Press, 1977.

Numbers, Ronald L., and Darrel W. Amundsen, eds. *Caring and Curing: Health and Medicine in the Western Religious Traditions*. New York: Macmillan, 1986.

Ostrow, David G., ed. *Behavioral Aspects of AIDS*. New York: Plenum Medical Book Co., 1990.

Parad, Howard J., and Libbie G. Parad. *Crisis Intervention, Book 2: The Practitioner's Sourcebook for Brief Therapy*. Milwaukee: Family Service America, 1990.

BIBLIOGRAPHY

Pastoral Care and Cancer. Chicago, Ill.: American Cancer Society, Illinois Division.

Paterson, George. *The Cardiac Patient.* Minneapolis: Augsburg Press, 1978.

Pruyser, Paul W. *The Minister As Diagnostician.* Philadelphia: Westminster Press, 1976.

Richmond, Kent D. *A Time to Die: A Handbook for Funeral Sermons.* Nashville: Abingdon Press, 1990.

————. *Preaching to Sufferers: God and the Problem of Pain.* Nashville: Abingdon Press, 1988.

Ritual in a New Day. Nashville: Abingdon, 1976.

Sarno, John E., and Martha Taylor Sarno, with Introduction by Howard A. Rusk. *Stroke: A Guide for Patients and Their Families.* New York: McGraw Hill, 1979.

Siegel, Bernie S. *Love, Medicine, and Miracles.* New York: Harper and Row, 1986.

Wicks, Robert J., Jeffrey A. Fine, and Jerome J. Platt, eds. *Crisis Intervention.* New York: Charles C. Slack, 1988.

Willimon, William H. *Worship As Pastoral Care.* Nashville: Abingdon, 1979.

Word and Table: A Basic Pattern of Sunday Worship for United Methodists. Nashville: Abingdon, 1976.

JOURNALS

Anderson, David. "Death and Dying: Ethics at the End of Life." *RN* (October 1988): 42-51.

Annas, George J. "Do Feeding Tubes Have More Rights Than Patients?" *The Hastings Center Report* (February 1986): 26-28.

Ballantine, H. Thomas, Jr. "Annual Discourse—The Crisis in Ethics, Anno Domini 1979." *The New England Journal of Medicine* (Sept. 20, 1979): 634-38.

Chapman, Carleton B. "On the Definition and Teaching of the Medical Ethic." *The New England Journal of Medicine* (Sept. 20, 1979): 630-34.

Clements, Colleen D., and Roger C. Sider. "Medical Ethics' Assault Upon Medical Values." *JAMA* 250 (Oct. 21, 1983): 2011-15.

Derry, Patrick G. "Why Food and Fluids Can Never Be Denied." *The Hastings Center Report* (February 1986): 28-30.

Dresser, Rebecca S., and Eugene V. Boisaubin, Jr. "Ethics, Law, and Nutritional Support." *Archives of Internal Medicine* 145 (January 1985): 122-24.

Gula, Richard M. "Moral Principles Shaping Public Policy on Euthanasia." *Second Opinion* 14 (July 1990): 73-83.

Lynn, Joanne, and James F. Childress. "Must Patients Always Be Given Food and Water?" *The Hastings Center Report* 13 (October 1983): 17-21.

Margolis, Joseph. "Conceptual Aspects of a Patient's Bill of Rights." *Connecticut Medicine* 39 (no. 9): 582-87.

Martyn, S., R. Wright, et al. "Required Request for Organ Donation: Moral, Clinical, and Legal Problems." *The Hastings Center Report* (April-May 1988): 27-34.

BIBLIOGRAPHY

Minogue, Brendan P. "The Exclusion of Theology from Public Policy: The Case of Euthanasia." *Second Opinion* 14 (July 1990): 85-93.

Mitchell, Kenneth R. "Ritual in Pastoral Care." *The Journal of Pastoral Care* 43 (Spring 1989): 68-77.

"The New Medical Ethics: A Second Opinion." *Archives of Internal Medicine* 145 (December 1985): 2169-71.

Norton, Daniel J. "Helping Patients Give the Gift of Life." *RN* (December 1990): 30-34.

Orentlicher, David. "Advance Medical Directives." *JAMA* 263 (May 2, 1990): 2365-67.

Otten, Allan L. "Can't We Put My Mother to Sleep?" *The Wall Street Journal.* June 5, 1985.

"Persistent Vegetative State and the Decision to Withdraw or Withhold Life Support." Council on Scientific Affairs and Council on Ethical and Judicial Affairs, *JAMA* 263 (Jan. 19, 1990): 426-30.

Prottas, Jeffrey, and Helen Levine Batten. "Health Professionals and Hospital Administrators in Organ Procurement: Attitudes, Reservations, and Their Resolutions." *American Journal of Public Health* 78 (June 1988): 642-45.

Ross, Judith Wilson, and Deborah Pugh. "Limited Cardiopulmonary Resuscitation: The Ethics of Partial Codes." *Quality Review Bulletin* (January 1988): 4-8.

Schiedermayer, David L. "Can Doctors Agree with God on the Time to Die?" *Christian Medical Society Journal* 17 (Summer 1986): 15-17.

Stolman, Cynthia J., et al. "Evaluation of the Do Not Resuscitate Orders at a Community Hospital." *Archives of Internal Medicine* 149 (August 1989): 1851-56.

Tillich, Paul. "The Theology of Pastoral Care." *Pastoral Psychology* 10 (October 1959).

Wanzer, Sidney, et al. "The Physician's Responsibility Toward Hopelessly Ill Patients." *The New England Journal of Medicine* 310 (no. 15): 955-59.

"Who Lives, Who Dies? Who Decides?" *American Medical News*, Chicago, Ill.: American Medical Society (Jan. 7, 1991).